∽Writers and Their Works∽

Mark Twain

Debra McArthur

Marshall Cavendish
Benchmark
New York

This book is gratefully dedicated to my mentor
and friend, Louise Hawes, for her kind words, gentle
spirit, and unwavering encouragement.

With thanks to Forrest Robinson, professor of
American Studies and Literature, University
of California, Santa Cruz, for his expert
review of this manuscript.

Marshall Cavendish Benchmark
99 White Plains Road
Tarrytown, NY 10591
www.marshallcavendish.us

Library of Congress Cataloging-in-Publication Data

McArthur, Debra.
Mark Twain / by Debra McArthur.
p. cm. — (Writers and their works)
Includes bibliographical references and index.
Summary: "A biography of writer Mark Twain, describing his life, his major
works, and the legacy of his writing"—Provided by publisher.
ISBN 0-7614-1950-0
1. Twain, Mark, 1835-1910. 2. Humorists, American—19th
century—Biography. 3. Authors, American—19th century—Biography. 4.
Journalists—United States—Biography. I. Title. II. Series.

PS1331.M225 2005
818'.409—dc22

2004025188

Photo research by Linda Sykes Picture Research, Inc., Hilton Head, SC

\The photographs in this book are used by permission and through the courtesy of:

Cover: Mark Twain House and Museum, Hartford, CT

Mark Twain House and Museum, Hartford, CT: 2, 23, 52 left, 52 right, 53, 71; The Granger
Collection: 8, 15, 19, 21, 24, 34, 47, 78, 81; Nevada Historical Society: 12; Mark Twain Project,
University of California, Berkeley: 29, 40, 56; Buffalo and Erie County Historical Society: 44;
American Antiquarian Society: 6; University of Virginia: 73, 93, 109; Library of Congress: 85.

Series design by Sonia Chaghatzbanian
Printed in China
135642

igh the trees. I went for it, cautious and slow. By and
ind. It most give me the fantods. He had a blanket arour
a clump of bushes in about six foot of him, and kept n
he gapped and stretched himself and hove off the bla
ays:

Contents

imself and hove off the blanket, and it was Miss Watso
Hello, Jim!" and skipped out.
Ie bounced up and stared at me wild. Then he drops dowr
Doan' hurt me -- don t! I hain't ever done no harm to a
n git in de river agin, whah you b'longs, en doan' do n
Vell, I warn't long making him understand I warn't dead
Varn't afraid of HIM telling the people where I was. I ta
ng. Then I says:
It's good daylight. Le's get breakfast. Make up your cam
What's de use er makin' up de camp fire to cook strawbrie
etter den strawbries."
Strawberries and such truck," I says. "Is that what you
I couldn' git nuffn else," he says. "Why, how long you be
What, all that time?"
Yes -- indeedy."
And ain't you had nothing but that kind of rubbage to
No, sah -- nuffn else."
Well, you must be most starved, ain't you?"
I reck'n I could eat a hoss. I think I could. How long y
Since the night I got killed."
But by and by, sure enough, I catched a glimpse of fire
was close enough to have a look, and there laid a man
is head, and his head was nearly in the fire. I set th
yes on him steady. It was getting gray daylight now. Pr
nd it was Miss Watson's Jim! I bet I was glad to see him
Hello, Jim!" and skipped out.
Ie bounced up and stared at me wild. Then he drops down
Doan' hurt me -- don t! I hain't ever done no harm to a
n git in de river agin, whah you b'longs, en doan' do nu
Vell, I warn't long making him understand I warn't dead
varn't afraid of HIM telling the people where I was. I ta
ng. Then I says:
It's good daylight. Le's get breakfast. Make up your camp
What's de use er makin' up de camp fire to cook strawbrie
etter den strawbries."
Strawberries and such truck," I says. "Is that what you
I couldn' git nuffn else," he says.
Why, how long you been on the island, Jim?"
I come heah de night arter you's killed."
What, all that time?"
Yes -- indeedy."
And ain't you had nothing but that kind of rubbage to

Part I:
The Life of
Samuel Clemens

MARK TWAIN LOVED HIS OXFORD ROBES, GIVEN TO HIM LATE IN LIFE WHEN HE RECEIVED HIS HONORARY DEGREE FROM OXFORD UNIVERSITY. HE LOVED THE SPLENDOR OF THE COLORS, AND WORE THEM OVER THE CLASSIC WHITE SUITS FOR WHICH HE WAS KNOWN.

Chapter 1

From Florida to Hannibal, Up and Down the Mississippi

"What a wee little part of a person's life are his acts and his words! His real life is led in his head, and is known to none but himself. . . . Biographies are but the clothes and buttons of the man—the biography of the man himself cannot be written."

Mark Twain

HE WAS A MAN WITH TWO NAMES for most of his life: Samuel Clemens and Mark Twain. In many ways, Samuel Clemens the man was very different from his alter ego, Mark Twain the writer. Samuel Clemens was born in the slaveholding state of Missouri, but Mark Twain chose to make his home in the Yankee state of Connecticut. Although Samuel Clemens made few trips back to his hometown, Mark Twain visited it again and again in his writings. Samuel Clemens loved to be at home surrounded by his family, but Mark Twain spent much of his time traveling in the United States and abroad as a lecturer. Samuel Clemens had very little formal education, but Mark Twain received honorary degrees from the University of Missouri, Yale University, and Oxford University in England. Samuel Clemens rejected organized religion, but Mark Twain could not resist it in his writing, and, even at his most satiric seemed to cling to a belief in a higher power.

"Mark was the noblest literary artist who ever set pen to paper on American soil, and not only the noblest artist, but also one of the most profound and sagacious philosophers."

—H. L. Mencken, 1913

In his writing Mark Twain was an outspoken critic of the institution of slavery, but Samuel Clemens volunteered in a militia unit that was formed to fight against Union troops at the beginning of the Civil War. Mark Twain made fun of America's wealthy class, but Samuel Clemens sought wealth throughout his life with pursuits ranging from gold prospecting to investing in inventions. Although Mark Twain's writing made him one of the wealthiest men in America, Samuel Clemens's pursuit of get-rich-quick schemes forced him to declare bankruptcy. Mark Twain achieved international success as a humorist, but Samuel Clemens endured great tragedy and a personal sense of guilt and failure through much of his life.

Although Samuel Clemens and Mark Twain may seem as unlike as two entirely different people, they are more like two sides of the same coin: presenting two different aspects of one remarkable man.

"Under the humorist in Mark Twain lies the keen observer, the serious man, the ardent reformer, and he took note of all that was evil in the life he knew and proclaimed it indignantly to the world."

—Charles Miner Thompson, 1897

The Autobiography of Mark Twain is one important source of interesting stories about Samuel Clemens and his life. Still, we cannot rely upon the book for the whole truth about Samuel Clemens's life. The book was intended for publication after his death, but some portions were published during his lifetime. Because of this, the autobiography contained a good measure of the humor for which Twain was known and portrayed an image of the writer that he wanted the world to see. He composed the book during the later years of his life, when he jokingly admitted, "When I was younger I could remember anything, whether it had happened or not; but my faculties are decaying now and soon I shall be so I cannot remember any but the things that never happened."

Samuel Clemens actually recalled the settings and people of his youth with great clarity. These were the same settings and people that would become important to his writings as Mark Twain.

Samuel Langhorn Clemens was the sixth of seven children born to John Marshall Clemens and Jane Lampton Clemens in the small town of Florida, Missouri. Samuel's father was a Southerner from Virginia who settled first in Kentucky, then in Tennessee, always searching for his path to riches. Clemens moved his family to the town of Florida in the early 1830s to join John Quarles, who was married to Jane's sister Patsy, in business in a general store there. Although the two men soon dissolved their business partnership, they remained friends. Quarles continued to prosper with his successful store, his growing plantation that included about thirty slaves, and even a hotel in nearby Paris, Missouri. Meanwhile, Clemens struggled to support his family in the town of only one hundred people.

Samuel was born on November 30, 1835, two months before he was due to arrive. He was so small that his family did not expect him to survive. He did, but was a sickly child. In his autobiography, Clemens writes that he spoke with his elderly mother many years later about the time when

JANE LAMPTON CLEMENS GAVE BIRTH TO SEVEN CHILDREN. SHE SURVIVED THE DEATH OF HER HUSBAND AND THREE CHILDREN BUT ALWAYS RETAINED A SUNNY DISPOSITION. SAMUEL CLEMENS, KNOWN TO HIS READERS AS MARK TWAIN, WAS THE SIXTH OF HER CHILDREN.

his survival was unsure. His story, if true, may give us a hint of Jane Clemens's own sense of humor.

> "I suppose that during all that time you
> were uneasy about me?"
> "Yes, the whole time."
> "Afraid I wouldn't live?"
> After a reflective pause—ostensibly to think
> out the facts— "No—afraid you would."

By 1839, John Clemens was sure he could never make a good living in Florida and moved the family to the growing town of Hannibal, Missouri. This change was important for four-year-old "Little Sammy" Clemens, as he was known by his family. The growing town of Hannibal offered new adventures for the little boy, as well as a collection of new friends who would later become main characters in Twain's fictional town of St. Petersburg in *The Adventures of Tom Sawyer* and *The Adventures of Huckleberry Finn*. It also placed him alongside the Mississippi River—the river that would become a source of fascination and inspiration for him.

Samuel attended several private schools during his early years in Hannibal, but he was a reluctant student. His first teacher was Mrs. Horr, and he disliked her strict rules and her eagerness to use a switch for correcting improper behavior. Even on his first day he managed to get into trouble. She sent him outdoors to find a switch with which she would administer his punishment. He came back with the most rotted stick he could find. He later recalled, "She said she would try and appoint a boy with better judgment than mine in the matter of switches, and it saddens me yet to remember how many faces lighted up with the hope of getting that appointment. Jim Dunlap got it and when he returned with the switch of his choice I recognized that he was an expert."

Life in Hannibal

"In the small town of Hannibal, Missouri, when I was a boy everybody was poor but didn't know it; and everybody was comfortable and did know it. And there were grades of society—people of good family, people of unclassified family, people of no family. Everybody knew everybody and was affable to everybody and nobody put on visible airs; yet the class lines were quite clearly drawn and the familiar social life of each class was restricted to that class. It was a little democracy full of liberty, equality, and Fourth of July, and sincerely so, too; yet you perceived that the aristocratic taint was there. It was there and nobody found fault with the fact or ever stopped to reflect that its presence was an inconsistency."

—Mark Twain

Although Samuel did not care for school and frequently found ways to avoid it, he did enjoy reading. His favorite books were adventure stories, and they often provided the inspiration for games of pirates and Robin Hood for Samuel and his friends. Much of this play would later find its way into Twain's books in the imaginative games of Tom Sawyer in both *The Adventures of Tom Sawyer* and *The Adventures of Huckleberry Finn*. Life along the river was also exciting for the boys, because the Mississippi had become a busy water highway with steady steamboat traffic. As he wrote later in *Life on the Mississippi*, "When I was a boy, there was but one permanent ambition among my comrades in our village . . . to be a steamboatsman. We had transient ambitions of other sorts, but they were only transient. . . .These ambitions faded out, each in its turn; but the ambition to be a steamboatsman always remained." The boys' games and adventures on the banks of the Mississippi River would become important elements in many of Twain's stories.

THE SMALL TOWN OF HANNIBAL, MISSOURI, ON THE MISSISSIPPI RIVER WHERE SAMUEL CLEMENS GREW UP, IS PICTURED HERE BY LITHOGRAPHIC ARTIST ALBERT RUGER IN 1869, SIXTEEN YEARS AFTER CLEMENS HAD MOVED AWAY. THE RIVER WOULD PROVIDE INSPIRATION—MANY TIMES OVER—FOR THE WRITER MARK TWAIN.

The move away from Florida, Missouri, did not end Samuel's association with it. His Uncle John Quarles and Aunt Patsy invited him to spend summers with them at their farm. There he had great freedom to explore the woods and fields with his cousins. They spent much of their time gathering berries, fishing, and eating well at his uncle's table. In his autobiography, Twain described the Quarles farm in great detail. In fact, his descriptions of the Quarles farm so closely resemble his description of the Grangerford house and grounds in *The Adventures of Huckleberry Finn*, it is clear he used his boyhood memories to create this fictional place. He also used many details from the Quarles farm in his description of the Phelps farm in that same book.

Mark Twain on Morality

When called upon to discuss morality, Twain often told the following story from his childhood days in Hannibal:

"One night I stole—I mean I removed—a watermelon from a wagon while the owner was attending to another customer. I crawled off to a secluded spot, where I found that it was green. It was the greenest melon in the Mississippi Valley. Then I began to reflect. I began to be sorry. I wondered what George Washington would have done had he been in my place. I thought a long time, and then suddenly felt that strange feeling that comes to a man with a good resolution, and took up that watermelon and took it back to its owner. I handed him the watermelon and told him to reform. He took my lecture much to heart, and, when he gave me a good one in place of the green melon, I forgave him."

—Mark Twain, 1902

Missouri was granted statehood in 1821. By that time, slavery was already well-established in Missouri, and it was admitted to the Union as a slave state. County property records indicate that Samuel's Uncle John Quarles owned about thirty slaves when Samuel was a boy, and Samuel and his cousins loved to spend time with them. He became well acquainted with the speech patterns, folklore, and customs of the slaves, whose companionship he enjoyed. Although the Quarles's slaves were treated more kindly than some, Samuel also saw the cruel aspects of slavery. When he was only ten, he witnessed the killing of a slave. He also knew that being "sold down the river" to the Southern plantations was the worst fate a Missouri slave might fear, because most people believed that the treatment of slaves was even more cruel in the states farther south. He once described a group of slaves at the dock in Hannibal awaiting shipment south as having, "the saddest faces I ever saw." Later, slavery would be an important issue in Twain's writing.

Slaves in the Clemens Household

Samuel's mother, Jane Lampton Clemens, was a product of Southern upbringing, and so accepted the institution of slavery as a natural part of the society in which she lived. When her slave, Jennie, acted up, Jane threatened her with a whip. Jennie snatched the whip from her hand. John Clemens punished Jennie by tying her wrists with a horse bridle and whipping her. But Samuel also remembered that his mother was sad about the tragedies that accompanied slave life. A young slave boy named Sandy worked for the Clemens family. The boy sang, whistled, and laughed as he went about his daily chores, and young Samuel disliked the constant noise. When he complained about it to his mother, she replied with tears in her eyes, "Poor thing, when he sings it shows that he is not remembering and that comforts me; but when he is still I am afraid he is thinking and I cannot bear it. He will never see his mother again; if he can sing I must not hinder it, but be thankful for it."

Even in Hannibal, John Clemens struggled to make a living for his family. He first opened a store, then worked as a lawyer, justice of the peace, and even a judge, but still failed to become financially successful. In 1847, Clemens was a candidate for county office, and appeared to be leading the race, but during the campaign, he became ill and died. It was a severe blow to the family. Samuel's older brother, Orion, worked in St. Louis and sent money home to help out. His sister Pamela gave piano lessons. Jane took boarders into their home for extra money, and eventually sold much of their property. Eleven-year-old Samuel took a position as a printer's apprentice for the local newspaper, the *Missouri Courier*. He did not receive any money for his work. The editor provided him with food and clothes, though not much of either. As he set the type for the newspaper stories, Samuel began to read the stories and think about the craft of writing.

In 1850, Orion Clemens returned to Hannibal and took over the publishing of the *Hannibal Western Union*. He hired Samuel to work for him and promised to pay him three dollars and fifty cents a week to do the typesetting. Later, Orion merged the *Western Union* with another newspaper, the *Hannibal Journal*. In addition to typesetting, Samuel began to write for the newspaper. In 1852, when his brother was out of town, he wrote a story in which he made fun of the editor of a rival newspaper. It made the man so angry that he burst into the newspaper office with a shotgun, threatening to kill Orion, whom he assumed had written the story. Finding that the writer was only a youngster, he pulled Sam's ears and left. Samuel wrote some short pieces about life and people in Hannibal. Several of his stories were even reprinted in some newspapers in Boston and Philadelphia. The writer was identified only as "SLC."

Samuel may have tried to stir up some controversy in order to boost sales. In 1853, Samuel contributed a poem

SAMUEL CLEMENS POSES AT AGE FIFTEEN. THIS IS THE EARLIEST KNOWN PORTRAIT OF HIM, BUT ALREADY HE SHOWS A SWAGGER AND STRONG SENSE OF SELF.

to the *Hannibal Journal* that he signed as "The Rambler." In editions that followed, letters commenting on the poem, signed with the name "The Grumbler" ran in the paper. These were followed by responses from "The Rambler," who denounced "Grumbler" as "ignorant" and wished him "safe arrival at that place for which only you are a fit subject—the Lunatic Asylum." Another letter signed "Peter Pencilcase's Son John Snooks" appeared a few days later, commenting on the letters by both "Rambler" and "Grumbler." C. J. Armstrong, a Hannibal minister who studied Twain's early writing, concluded that Samuel wrote all these letters, probably to try to liven up the paper and increase readership. Despite his efforts, the paper was still not successful, and Orion never actually made enough money to pay his brother.

In 1853, Samuel felt he needed a change. At age seventeen, he left home after promising his mother he would stay away from drinking and gambling. Samuel worked as a typesetter in New York and Philadelphia and continued to write. He also sent some articles back to Hannibal for publication in Orion's newspaper. Orion married and left Hannibal with his bride. Sam's mother and younger brother Henry moved along with Orion, settling in the town of Keokuk, Iowa. In 1854, Samuel returned to his family. He agreed to work with Orion in his print shop, but again, Orion made so little money that he could not pay Samuel even the small salary he had promised. Samuel did not stay long. He took his first real writing job for the *Keokuk Post*, writing travel letters at a rate of five dollars each. He spent the next few years traveling around the Midwest.

In 1857, at the age of twenty-one, Clemens was ready to embark on a new quest to make his fortune. He had heard of a miraculous plant in South America, rumored to have extraordinary powers to give a person energy and strength. He planned to establish a trade in this new product—the coca plant. He booked passage on the riverboat *Paul Jones* to

SAMUEL CLEMENS WAS ISSUED HIS PILOT'S CERTIFICATE ON APRIL 9, 1859. HE WORKED AS A RIVERBOAT PILOT UNTIL THE CIVIL WAR, BEGUN IN 1861, STOPPED ALL RIVERBOAT TRAFFIC.

HENRY CLEMENS, SAM'S YOUNGER BROTHER, WAS BADLY HURT AS A RESULT OF A JUNE 16, 1858, EXPLOSION ON THE STEAMBOAT *PENNSYLVANIA*, AND SUBSEQUENTLY DIED WHEN A DOCTOR GAVE HIM AN OVERDOSE OF MORPHINE. SAM CLEMENS NEVER GOT OVER HIS GUILT AT HAVING GOTTEN HIS BROTHER A JOB ON THE BOAT, EVEN THOUGH HIS BROTHER'S DEATH WAS IN NO WAY HIS FAULT.

New Orleans, intending to go to Brazil from there. On his way down the Mississippi, he became acquainted with the pilot of the boat, Horace Bixby. Bixby allowed Clemens to steer the boat during the days, and the old dream of being a riverboat pilot came back to him. On arrival in New Orleans, Clemens learned that no ships were headed to Brazil from there. He persuaded Bixby to take him on as an apprentice.

This was the life he had dreamed of since his boyhood in Hannibal, and he loved his new career. He was also paid well, at last earning a regular salary. In the spring of 1858, Clemens was twenty-two years old and earning $250 a month on the *Pennsylvania*, which made trips between St. Louis and New Orleans. He helped his younger brother Henry get a job on the boat, but during one evening when the boat was in port in St. Louis, Samuel had a disturbing dream. "In the dream I had seen Henry a corpse. He lay in a metallic burial case. He was dressed in a suit of my clothing and on his breast lay a great bouquet of flowers, mainly white roses, with a red rose in the center."

On the trip to New Orleans, Samuel Clemens had a disagreement with his boss and was fired and put ashore. Henry continued the voyage, and Samuel followed on another boat the next day. Soon, news reached Samuel's boat that the boilers on the *Pennsylvania* had exploded and several people were badly hurt. Arriving in Memphis, he found Henry in the hospital, near death. Although Henry seemed to be recovering a week later, he was given an accidental overdose of morphine by the doctor on duty and died. When Samuel returned to claim his brother's body, he found Henry had been dressed in a suit of Sam's clothes and placed in a metal casket. Samuel recalled his dream, but realized there was still a detail missing. "Just then an elderly lady entered the place with a large bouquet consisting

IN *LIFE ON THE MISSISSIPPI*, MARK TWAIN WOULD LOVINGLY REVISIT THE DAYS WHEN SAMUEL CLEMENS WAS A RIVERBOAT PILOT.

mainly of white roses, and in the center of it was a red rose and she laid it on his breast." Clemens felt great guilt for his brother's death. He had helped him get the job; he had left Henry alone on the *Pennsylvania*; he had been present when the doctor gave Henry the overdose. Although no one else would blame him for the series of events that led to Henry's death, it was a burden he would always carry.

Clemens continued to work as a riverboat pilot for nearly two more years. He learned the secrets of the river, including its landmarks and hidden dangers. It was still a very good living, and he was even able to send money to help his brother Orion, whose business was struggling. It was a wonderful life, but it could not last. The beginning of the Civil War in 1861 stopped all commercial traffic on the Mississippi. It would mark the beginning of a new chapter in the life of Samuel Clemens.

Chapter 2

To the West and Beyond

LIKE MANY OTHER YOUNG MEN, Clemens prepared to take part in the war. He returned to Hannibal and, together with some of his boyhood friends, organized a militia unit called the Marion Rangers. According to Albert Bigelow Paine's account, the main goal of the small company was to avoid meeting the enemy. After two weeks, the group broke up. Some of the others joined the regular Confederate army. Clemens had already decided that he did not want any part of the fighting. He was ready to look for adventure far away from the battlefields, although he would always be troubled by the question of whether this decision was motivated by good sense or cowardice.

Samuel's brother Orion was still struggling to succeed in business. By this time, his newspaper had failed and he was trying to work as a lawyer in Alexandria, Iowa. Samuel supported Orion for several months with money he had saved from his riverboat days. Eventually, Orion's political connections with a member of President Lincoln's cabinet earned him a better opportunity.

In 1861, Orion was named secretary of the Territory of Nevada. Orion looked forward to the political appointment, but did not have the money for the stagecoach trip. Samuel envied Orion's opportunity to travel in the West. He offered to pay the stagecoach fare if Orion would take him along. Orion hired his brother to serve as his personal secretary. As in his previous work for his brother, Samuel received no pay, but then, the job of secretary to the secretary carried few duties. Most important, it was an opportunity to get away from the war.

Samuel Clemens, Confederate Soldier

When the Civil War broke out, many of the young men of Hannibal made plans to defend their home state from the "Union invaders" by forming small militia groups. When Clemens arrived back home after losing his job on the riverboat, several of his boyhood chums were banding together to join the Confederacy. They were outfitted with a few supplies, guns, a mule, and some horses, all contributed by local farmers. According to biographer Albert Bigelow Paine, the Marion Rangers went about their soldiering, "just as Tom Sawyer's band might have done if it had thought of playing 'War,' instead of 'Indian' and 'Pirate' and 'Bandit' with fierce raids on peach orchards and melon patches." After camping in the rain for days, riding a mule that preferred to wade instead of swim a deep river, developing a painful boil in a place that made sitting in the saddle extremely uncomfortable, and surviving a barn fire set by careless smoking, Clemens decided he would leave the war to others. In his autobiography he wrote, "I resigned after two weeks' service in the field, explaining that I was 'incapacitated by fatigue' through persistent retreating." In an embellished account of the experience, entitled "The Private History of a Campaign that Failed," Twain wrote, "I could have become a soldier myself, if I had waited. I had part of it learned; I knew more about retreating than the man that invented retreating."

Samuel Clemens went with a friend to Lake Tahoe, where they laid claim to a wooded area and thought they would make their fortunes in timber. They enjoyed camping at the beautiful site at the water's edge, but one night their campfire got away from them and destroyed it all. He would have to make his fortune some other way.

Like many others in the territory, Clemens was lured by the promise of wealth. Although the 1848 gold rush had drawn many prospectors to California, in 1859 the lure of silver drew them to Nevada. Clemens traveled from one area to another, staking claims on prospective silver mines, but finding each to be worthless. Again and again his hopes were raised and his fortune seemed secure, but each time he found himself defeated and faced with more debt. Although most of his letters to Orion contained requests for investment money to continue the mining, they also contained lively and entertaining stories of his adventures. Orion showed some of these letters to an editor of the Virginia City *Territorial Enterprise*. The editor liked them, and asked for more. Clemens wrote these humorous pieces under the pen name of "Josh," and the newspaper continued to print them.

By the fall of 1862, Clemens knew it was time to make a decision. None of the mining claims had been profitable, and Orion's small salary could no longer support them. With the Civil War still raging, Samuel did not want to go back East. His letters in the *Enterprise* had been a success, though, and the newspaper offered him a job in Virginia City as a reporter for the newspaper at a salary of twenty-five dollars a week. Orion stayed in the territorial capital of Carson City.

Virginia City was growing quickly because of the rich silver mines in the area, and the newspaper was also growing. Samuel enjoyed the life of a reporter in the bustling town, and quickly gained a reputation for his humorous pieces. As in his younger days, Clemens signed his writing with fictitious names. In February 1863, he found a new identity: he began to sign his stories with the name "Mark

Twain." The term was the call of the riverboat pilot to indicate a water depth of two fathoms or twelve feet. For the pilot, twelve feet was the depth at which safe channel water became dangerously shallow water. "Mark Twain" was soon to become a public character, separate and apart from Samuel Clemens. This dual identity would continue throughout the rest of his life.

As a writer, Twain also hovered at that precarious spot between safe and dangerous journalism. He made fun of local politicians and other writers, and his writing become popular enough to be reprinted in newspapers in California and back East. Some of his subjects did not find his work so funny, however. In the spring of 1864, Twain wrote a story accusing a local women's society of collecting money to contribute to a group promoting marriage between people of different races. He next published an attack on the employees of a competing newspaper. When Clemens was challenged to a duel, he decided this would be a good time for a change of scenery.

His next stop was San Francisco. Here he enjoyed a life of high society and the company of other writers, such as Ambrose Bierce and Bret Harte. He dressed well, ate well, drank well, and worked for the *Morning Call* newspaper.

All That Glitters

Twain's 1872 book, *Roughing It*, contained his memories of (and commentary on) his "Western adventures" in the years 1862–1865, and also included stories of his later trip to the Sandwich Islands (later renamed Hawaii). In Chapter 28, Twain recalls his early days of prospecting when he planned to make his fortune in the silver mines. One day he discovered gold-colored bits on the bottom of a stream bed and filled his pockets with them. When he showed them to a local prospector, however, he was disappointed to find that the treasure was not gold, but merely glittery mica. He recounts:

> So vanished my dream. So melted my wealth away. So toppled my airy castle to the earth and left me stricken and forlorn.
>
> Moralizing, I observed, then, that "all that glitters is not gold."
>
> Mr. Ballou said I could go further than that, and lay it up among my treasures of knowledge, that *nothing* that glitters is gold. So I learned then, once and for all, that gold in its native state is but dull, unornamental stuff, and that only low-born metals excite the admiration of the ignorant with an ostentatious glitter. However, like the rest of the world, I still go on underrating men of gold and glorifying men of mica. Commonplace human nature cannot rise above that.

Despite this "moralizing," Clemens did not apply this important lesson later in life, and several times suffered the consequences of pursuing apparently "golden" business opportunities that turned out to be only "mica."

Traveling West with the Clemenses

The trip West by stagecoach was a memorable experience for the Clemenses. When they left for the West, Samuel and Orion did not know what they would find in the territory, but they were certain they would not be able to find a good dictionary.

Edward Bates, then a member of Mr. Lincoln's first Cabinet, got [Orion] the place of Secretary of the new Territory of Nevada, and Orion and I cleared for that country in the overland stagecoach, I paying the fares, which were pretty heavy, and carrying with me what money I had been able to save—this was eight hundred dollars, I should say—and it was all in silver coin and a good deal of a nuisance because of its weight. And we had another nuisance, which was an Unabridged Dictionary. It weighed about a thousand pounds and was a ruinous expense, because the stagecoach company charged for extra baggage by the ounce. We could have kept a family for a time on what that dictionary cost in the way of extra freight—and it wasn't a good dictionary, anyway—didn't have any modern words in it—only had obsolete ones that they used to use when Noah Webster was a child.

—Mark Twain

He also was able to write more pieces for a literary magazine called the *Golden Era*. While he enjoyed the company of Harte and others who wrote for the *Era*, he disliked his job at the *Call*, because he was not allowed to use his satire to criticize those in political power. The *Call* would not run a story in which he exposed corruption in the San Francisco police department. After only a few months there, Twain resigned. Although he was without his job at the *Call*, he was still sending letters to the *Enterprise* in Virginia City. He also submitted some articles to a literary magazine in San Francisco, *The Californian*, but those paychecks were

On Honesty and Bowling

"The proverb says that Providence protects children and idiots. This is really true. I know because I have tested it."

—Mark Twain

During his days in San Francisco, Clemens was invited by his fellow workers to join them for an evening of bowling. When he told them he didn't know anything about the game, they insisted he join them anyway. It was only after the group arrived at the bowling alley that the young men explained to Clemens that the loser would have to buy oysters and beer for the rest of the crowd after the game. They thought they had surely found easy prey in Clemens, who claimed he had never played before. After they explained the game to him and showed him how to roll the ball, Clemens was as surprised as the rest when every ball he rolled resulted in a strike. "The boys surrendered at the end of the half-hour and put on their coats and gathered around me and in courteous but sufficiently definite language expressed their opinion of an experience-worn and seasoned expert who would stoop to lying and deception in order to rob kind and well-meaning friends who had put their trust in him under the delusion that he was an honest and honorable person." After a few minutes, the alley owner explained to them that the alley Clemens used had a groove down the middle which would always lead the ball to a perfect hit on the head pin, no matter how it was thrown. Even after the explanation, however, Clemens was not entirely forgiven. "[I]t was ever thus, all through my life," he complained. "Whenever I have diverged from custom and principle and uttered a truth, the rule has been that the hearer hadn't strength of mind enough to believe it."

not steady. He lost money on the investments he had in silver mines, and, now deeply in debt, decided it was time to leave San Francisco.

After he left *The Enterprise* in October 1864, Clemens was invited to spend some time in a mining camp in Calaveras County, California. Although he did not spend much of his time looking for gold, he did spend time reading and writing in his journal. During this otherwise dull period for him, he heard one of the miners tell a tale about a man who bet on everything, including the jumping abilities of his pet frog. Later he turned the miner's tale into a story called "Jim Smiley and his Jumping Frog," and sent it to a friend in New York.

After three months in the camps, Clemens returned to San Francisco. He again worked as a reporter for *The Enterprise.* In the meantime, his friend had sent his story of the jumping frog to *The Saturday Press*, a magazine in New York. It was immediately popular and was reprinted in many newspapers across the country as "The Celebrated Jumping Frog of Calaveras County." In a letter to his mother, Clemens was quick to note that it was the frog who had become celebrated and not himself. He decided to stay in California, and soon got a job working for the *Sacramento Union*. In March 1866, the newspaper sent him on a four-month trip to the Sandwich Islands, on assignment to send back travel letters for the newspaper.

Readers enjoyed Twain's humorous pieces, and when he returned to San Francisco, a friend encouraged him to use his storytelling talents before live audiences as a lecturer. He rented a hall for the evening of October 2, 1866, and put out advertisements all over town that announced the lectures and added, "Doors open at 7 o'clock. The Trouble is to begin at 8 o'clock." He did not expect that anyone would come, but the night turned out to be a success and earned him more than a month's salary in his days as a riverboat pilot. He continued traveling through California and Nevada lecturing for the next month. Despite his popularity on stage and the money he made, he never really liked the lecture circuit. Still, it increased his fame and recognition. Mark Twain was suddenly famous,

Mark Twain on Stage Fright

In 1906, Twain addressed an audience that was present to hear his daughter Clara sing. He recalled his first time on the lecture stage in San Francisco:

> "I recall the occasion of my first appearance. . . . I got to the theatre forty-five minutes before the hour of the lecture. My knees were shaking so that I didn't know whether I could stand up. If there is an awful, horrible malady in the world, it is stage-fright—and seasickness. . . . I had stage fright then for the first and last time. . . . At last I began. . . . walked up and down—I was young in those days and needed the exercise—and talked and talked. . . .Well, after the first agonizing five minutes, my stage-fright left me, never to return. I know if I was going to be hanged I could get up and make a good showing, and I intend to. But I shall never forget my feelings before the agony left me, and I got up here to thank you for her for helping my daughter, by your kindness, to live through her first appearance. And I want to thank you for your appreciation of her singing, which is, by the way, hereditary."

and Samuel Clemens was at last successful. He had come a long way since leaving the Mississippi River. The Civil War was now over, and he was eager to return to the eastern states. It was time to move on once again, and the next step would have to be a big one.

The spring of 1867 found Clemens in the city where he most wanted to make a name for himself: New York. Twain's first book, *The Celebrated Jumping Frog of*

THE CELEBRATED JUMPING FROG OF CALAVERAS COUNTY AND OTHER SKETCHES, 1867, WAS MARK TWAIN'S FIRST PUBLICATION.

Calaveras County and Other Sketches, appeared in print as well. He made a brief trip back to Hannibal and was treated like a celebrity. He wrote letters back to the *Alta California,* but was soon restless again and eager to move on. On June 8, 1867, he left New York on the steamship *Quaker City,* bound for Europe and the Middle East. The trip was arranged by Rev. Henry Ward Beecher's Plymouth Church in Brooklyn, New York, and was intended to educate the travelers and enhance their spiritual lives. The Holy Land of the Bible was their destination, with stops throughout Europe along the way. Twain was sponsored by the *Alta California* to send travel letters back to the newspaper.

Most of the travelers were wealthy members of Beecher's church. Twain was hired to tell about the places they visited, but he told his travel story from the viewpoint of the common man, not through the eyes of a wealthy tourist. In fact, he wrote much about his religious "high society" fellow travelers, their reliance on their tourist guidebooks, and their prejudices toward the native people in the foreign lands they visited. As he said in the preface,

> This book is a record of a pleasure trip. . . . [I]t has a purpose, which is to suggest to the reader how *he* would be likely to see Europe and the East if he looked at them with his own eyes instead of the eyes of those who traveled in those countries before him. . . . I offer no apologies for any departures from the usual style of travel-writing that may be charged against me—for I think I have seen with impartial eyes, and I am sure I have written at least honestly, whether wisely or not.

California readers enjoyed Twain's humor, and by the time the group returned, Twain was well-known.

Pilgrims in Nazareth

Twain referred to himself and his fellow travelers as "pilgrims." His satire often focused on the prejudices among the group toward the people they met in other lands. As the group explored the area around the ancient city of Nazareth, Twain made fun of their reliance on their guidebooks and their fear of the local people:

> Some of us will be shot before we finish this pilgrimage. The pilgrims read "Nomadic Life" and keep themselves in a constant state of Quixotic heroism. They have their hands on their pistols all the time, and every now and then, when you least expect it, they snatch them out and take aim at Bedouins who are not visible, and draw their knives and make savage passes at other Bedouins who do not exist. . . . If the pilgrims would take deliberate aim and shoot at a man, it would be all right and proper—because that man would not be in any danger; but these random assaults are what I object to. I do not mind Bedouins, —I am not afraid of them; because neither Bedouins nor ordinary Arabs have shown any disposition to harm us, but I do feel afraid of my own comrades.

After the trip, Clemens settled down in Washington to an unsatisfying job as secretary to Nevada Senator William M. Stewart, but wanted to turn his many notes and letters into a book called *Innocents Abroad*. The *Alta* insisted that it owned the rights to all Twain's written material about the trip, so he went back to San Francisco to arrange a deal under which he could write and sell the book. Once the legal difficulties were resolved, Twain wrote the manuscript and had his friend, writer Bret Harte, help him trim and edit it. *Innocents Abroad* was sold by subscription across the United States and allowed Twain to engage in another successful lecture tour throughout the West.

Subscription Book Sales

Twain began his career writing for the American Publishing Company of Hartford, Connecticut. Instead of selling books to bookstores, American had subscription agents who sold their books door-to-door throughout the country. Subscription books were not considered literary, and most of the buyers were working-class people who had only modest education. The more literary authors of the day, such as Ralph Waldo Emerson and Henry Wadsworth Longfellow, would not write for a subscription publisher. Because of the relatively high price of a book, buyers expected a lot of pages for their money. This often required writers to pad their writing to fill up the required number of pages. Despite their poor literary reputation, subscription books sold well and provided good money for an author. Elisha Bliss, the secretary and managing director of the company, called the subscription book "the people's book." He was ready to market Twain as "the people's author."

He finished the tour in July 1868, and was ready to return to New York. By then, he had a new interest to pursue there: the younger sister of his friend Charles Langdon. Langdon and Clemens had met on the *Quaker City* voyage. Langdon had shown his new friend a small portrait of his younger sister Olivia. Clemens met Olivia on a brief trip to New York in December 1867, and the two attended a lecture by the English writer Charles Dickens together. Now he was determined to win the affection of the lovely young lady whom he would soon call "Livy."

SMALL CLEMENS FELL IN LOVE WITH OLIVIA LANGDON WHEN THEY FIRST MET; IT TOOK TWO YEARS TO WOO HER AND WIN HER PARENTS' APPROVAL FOR THE MATCH.

Chapter 3

The Family Man and the Writer

MARK TWAIN'S SUCCESS AND FAME as a writer and lecturer did not impress the Langdon family of Elmira, New York. Jervis Langdon had made a fortune in the coal industry and was one of the wealthiest and most respected men in town. The Langdons were educated, cultured, and religious. Charley's stories of his adventures with Clemens on the *Quaker City*, which included playing cards, drinking, and smoking, did not paint a picture of a man who would fit into Elmira society. Their daughter Olivia was beautiful, but had been in fragile health for years, and seldom had the strength to walk more than a few hundred yards. The Langdons were not convinced that Clemens was a suitable match for Olivia. Still, Clemens could not resist her charm and gentleness.

After their first meeting in December 1867, Clemens returned to the Langdon house for a visit the next August. He enjoyed his stay and told Charley of his affection for Olivia. After a carriage accident in Elmira, Clemens pretended to be injured and managed to stretch his stay at the Langdons' an extra three days. By the time the visit was over, Clemens knew that he wanted to make Olivia his wife.

Olivia did not approve of Clemens's drinking and smoking, nor of his evident lack of religious faith. She refused his proposal, but agreed to write to him. She insisted, however, that their affection be no more than that of a brother and sister. Clemens began to write to Olivia several times a week. As they had agreed, each letter was sealed and mailed in an envelope addressed to her brother

Clemens Extends His Stay

At the end of his visit to the Langdon house in August 1868, Clemens had his trunk packed and loaded into a wagon for the trip to the train station. When the Langdons' coachman snapped his whip to get the horse started, the animal lurched forward, tossing Clemens and Charley Langdon over the back of the wagon to the ground. Although Clemens was not hurt, he recognized his opportunity to stay a few extra days in the presence of Olivia Langdon. "I struck exactly on the top of my head and stood up that way for a moment, then crumbled down to the earth unconscious," he wrote in his autobiography. "It was a very good unconsciousness for a person who had not rehearsed the part. . . . I got not a bruise. I was not even jolted. Nothing was the matter with me at all." In an effort to make him feel better, Livy rubbed his head with medicine. According to Clemens, "That was very pleasant. I should have been obliged to recover presently if it hadn't been for that. But under Livy's manipulations—if they had continued—I should probably be unconscious to this day." Despite the family doctor, who insisted he was fine, Clemens managed to stretch his stay an extra three days. It was three days he used to try to convince Livy to marry him. "It helped a good deal," he said. "It pushed my suit forward several steps. A subsequent visit completed the matter and we became engaged conditionally; the condition being that the parents should consent."

Charley, so that neither the postman nor the neighbors would have reason to gossip.

Once Olivia relented and agreed to become engaged, Clemens's next hurdle was to convince Jervis Langdon he was good enough to marry Livy. Langdon agreed, on the condition that the engagement be kept secret until Clemens could provide suitable character references. Clemens's friends in the West described his worst character flaws to Jervis Langdon and strongly cautioned him against allowing his daughter to marry him. In his autobiography, Twain said, "The results were not promising. All those men were frank to a fault. They not only spoke in disapproval of me but they were unnecessarily and exaggeratedly enthusiastic about it." This sounds like Twain's typical humor, but, although it may be exaggerated, most biographers accept it as truth. Fortunately, Langdon had grown to like Clemens. In February 1869, he gave his blessing to the engagement of Clemens to this daughter.

The couple were married a year later, on February 2, 1870. As a wedding gift, Jervis Langdon bought the newlyweds a large and elegant house in Buffalo, New York. Clemens became part owner of the *Buffalo Express* newspaper, and seemed to be settling down to a happy and prosperous life. Soon, however, tragedy invaded their life. Jervis Langdon became ill and died in August 1870. Livy was pregnant, and her grief over her father's death brought her near to collapse. Her closest friend came to take care of her, but was herself ill with typhus and died at their home. Livy contracted the disease and gave birth too soon to a son the couple named Langdon. He was small and sickly from birth, but Clemens blamed himself for the child's illnesses because he had neglected to cover him well on a carriage ride. In March 1871, Clemens sold the Buffalo house and his interest in the newspaper and moved with Livy and baby Langdon to Hartford, Connecticut.

SAMUEL AND OLIVIA CLEMENS STARTED THEIR MARRIED LIFE IN STYLE WITH THE GIFT FROM HER FATHER OF A BEAUTIFUL HOUSE ON FASHIONABLE DELAWARE AVENUE IN BUFFALO. THEY LIVED THERE FOR ONLY A YEAR, HOWEVER, BEFORE MOVING TO HARTFORD, CONNECTICUT.

They rented a house in a fashionable neighborhood, and Clemens went on another lecture tour to raise the money to pay their debts and build a new house. He also continued work on *Roughing It*, a book about his days in Nevada and California and his trip to the Sandwich Islands. *Roughing It* was published in February 1872. According to biographer Albert Bigelow Paine, it sold nearly forty thousand copies in the first three months, reassuring Twain that he could still write a profitable book. The money from the lecture tour and the continued sales of *Innocents Abroad* also helped to ease their financial trouble. In March 1872, Livy gave birth to a healthy daughter, Olivia Susan, later nicknamed Susy, but the family endured more tragedy when twenty-month-old Langdon died just three months after Susy was born.

Just a few weeks after Langdon's death, Clemens began a tour of England. Twain's books had been copied and published all over England, so he was already quite popular there. Although he had gone with the intent of writing a satire of British culture, he found that he liked Britain so well that he could find nothing to satirize. When he came back to the United States, however, he found plenty to make fun of in America. Rumors of scandal and greed in Washington surrounded the presidency of Ulysses S. Grant.

American society seemed obsessed with wealth. Twain had an idea for a novel with a main character who would pursue an endless string of get-rich-quick schemes. He did not have confidence in his ability to complete a novel, however, so he asked for help from his friend and new neighbor Charles Dudley Warner. Together they wrote the novel called *The Gilded Age*. The main character, Colonel Sellers, was patterned after Clemens's cousin, James Lampton, who was always convinced that his fortune was just one scheme away. Through its ridicule of Sellers and his love of wealth, the writers portrayed the greed that seemed to be taking over American society. It was an immediate success, selling out three printings in the first month. Samuel Clemens, however, was as caught up in the quest for riches as anyone.

By 1873, the lecture tours and books were bringing in enough money for Samuel and Livy to purchase a large plot of ground in Hartford and hire an architect to build their dream home. It would be one of the largest and most elaborate houses in Hartford. While it was under construction in the spring of 1874, the Clemens family moved in with the family of Livy's sister, who lived on a farm near Elmira. Livy gave birth to another daughter, Clara, that summer. As a surprise for Clemens, Livy's sister had a hilltop writing retreat built. It was a small octagonal building on the top of a hill with a magnificent view. It became his favorite place, and he soon entered into one of the most productive writing phases of his life. Even after the new home was built, the Clemens family would go back to Quarry Farm every summer for nearly twenty years.

During the summer of 1874 at Quarry Farm, Twain began work on one of the most famous of all his works: *The Adventures of Tom Sawyer*. He began to recall his childhood experiences in Hannibal, which he named St. Petersburg for the book. Tom Sawyer played the role of young Samuel Clemens, with all the humor, mischief, and imagination that the author's own boyhood had contained. Many Hannibal personalities populated St. Petersburg, including his childhood sweetheart, Laura Hawkins, named Becky Thatcher in the book. Tom Blankenship, the son of Hannibal's only "Town Drunkard" in those days, according to Twain, became Huckleberry Finn in the novel. As he got to the end of the book, Twain was faced with a dilemma. How would he end the story? He showed

Twain's *The Gilded Age*, a satirical novel, was meant to make fun of the corruption that was rampant in Washington, D.C., during the administration of President Ulysses S. Grant, here savaged in an 1880 cartoon by Joseph Keppler.

the story to his friend, literary critic and author William Dean Howells, and asked his advice. Howells assured Twain the book worked best as a novel for boys, so Tom Sawyer did not need to grow into manhood at the end. Livy agreed, and Twain was persuaded to let Tom remain forever a boy.

Babies

In 1879, Twain gave a speech which probably described the Clemens household in those days when Susy and Clara were young:

> It is a shame that for a thousand years the world's banquets have utterly ignored the baby, as if he didn't amount to anything. . . . The idea that a baby doesn't amount to anything! Why, one baby is just a house and front yard full by itself. One baby can furnish more business than you and your whole Interior Department can attend to. He is enterprising, irrepressible, brimful of lawless activities. Do what you please, you can't make him stay on the reservation. Sufficient unto the day is one baby. As long as you are in your right mind don't you ever pray for twins. Twins amount to a permanent riot. And there ain't any real difference between triplets and an insurrection.
> —Mark Twain

The new home in Hartford was a magnificent structure with nineteen rooms, including a billiards room, and several large decks and porches. It was expensive to build and maintain. Livy needed hired help to assist her with the housework and the children. *The Adventures of Tom Sawyer*, published in 1876, was reviewed favorably by the critics and was liked by both children and adults, but did not sell as well as hoped. Clemens began work on a second novel of boyhood adventure that summer at Quarry Farm, featuring Tom's friend Huckleberry Finn. He wrote out about four hundred manuscript pages, but was not satisfied with the story and set it aside.

The years 1876–1879 included a number of disappointments for Clemens. He wanted to be accepted into the serious literary world of New England, but his unsophisticated and humorous style of writing was often not taken seriously by the critics of the day. Several plays were failures. He had begun several books but was having trouble finishing them. Meanwhile, the continuing costs of the Hartford house were becoming a burden, and Livy's health was suffering. A few months after an embarrassing incident at a literary gathering in honor of John Greenleaf Whittier's seventieth birthday, the family left for Europe on a trip that would keep them away from home for nearly a year and a half.

Twain was working on a book about his European travel experiences, *A Tramp Abroad*, but was struggling to finish it. Although he had hoped to accomplish a great deal of writing while abroad, he tore up nearly as many pages as he wrote. When the family came back to the United States in September 1879, both Samuel and Livy were glad to be home. That winter was hard on the family, as Livy was having a difficult pregnancy.

Daughter Jean was born in 1880, and life began to improve for the Clemens family. *A Tramp Abroad* had

Whittier's Birthday

In December 1877, Mark Twain was asked to speak at a dinner in Boston given by the publishers of *The Atlantic Monthly* in honor of poet John Greenleaf Whittier's seventieth birthday. Many writers of the day were invited to the event, including Henry Wadsworth Longfellow, Ralph Waldo Emerson, and Oliver Wendell Holmes. Along with Whittier they were considered among the finest and most dignified of writers in the nation, the youngest of whom was Holmes, at age sixty-eight. Twain prepared a humorous sketch for the occasion. He described a scene in a mining camp in Nevada where Holmes, Emerson, and Longfellow invaded a miner's cabin, spouting poetry and engaging in a drunken card game. They begin cheating and then throwing punches, until finally guns and knives are drawn. Twain punctuated the story with misquoted lines of poetry from the three, expecting that the poets and everyone else in the room would delight in the joke and find it wonderfully humorous. Instead, as he later recalled, "the expression of interest in the faces turned to a sort of black frost . . . . I went on with this awful performance, and carried it clear through to the end, in front of a body of people who seemed turned to stone with horror." Twain's friend William Dean Howells remembered the scene similarly. "There fell a silence, weighing many tons to the square inch, which deepened from moment to moment. . . . I stole a glance at [Clemens], and saw him standing solitary amid his appalled and appalling listeners, with his joke dead on his hands."

The local newspapers picked up the story the following morning, and called the speech, "in bad taste and out of place." Clemens wrote apologies to Emerson, Longfellow, and Holmes, and despaired of the event for months. At this event with the top literary personalities in America, he had fallen flat on his face. How much of Twain's account of it is exaggerated? Some historians have concluded that the event was not as dramatic as Twain and Howells described it, and that some in the audience, including the authors, did laugh at the story.

been published and was selling well. Twain's other novels were selling reasonably well and generating income, but more money was coming in from Twain's invention, the self-pasting scrapbook. Twain had patented a scrapbook with glue applied to the pages. When the pages were dampened, newspaper clippings, photos, and other items could be easily attached. It would turn out to be his only profitable invention.

Clemens enjoyed his time with the family at home. Livy and the girls listened to the new stories he wrote, and often offered suggestions. Livy helped edit the books, and the children were sometimes dismayed when she struck out some part they enjoyed. In 1881, he tried a different type of book: a children's historical novel set in England, *The Prince and the Pauper*. Susy was convinced that it was the best book her father had written so far. Critics liked the new book with its more formal language, and Clemens himself was pleased to break away from the type of humor for which he had become known.

The following year, Clemens took a steamboat trip traveling the length of the Mississippi River. It was his first return to the river since the Civil War. He added his new impressions of the river to his earlier memories to complete the manuscript for his book *Life on the Mississippi*. When he returned to his retreat at Quarry Farm in the summer of 1882, Twain was ready to finish his new book. That winter he also returned to his manuscript about Huckleberry Finn. By the end of his summer at Quarry Farm in 1883, he had finished the draft of the book.

Life on the Mississippi was published in May 1883. Twain was also involved in several other projects, including stories, plays, and a board game he had created. But the United States went into an economic slump in 1884, and Clemens's debts forced him to embark on another

Susy's Biography of Mark Twain

When Susy Clemens was about twelve years old, she began writing a biography of her father. In it, she tells about their family and her famous father.

> We are a very happy family. We consist of Papa, Mamma, Jean, Clara, and me. It is papa I am writing about, and I shall have no trouble in not knowing what to say about him, as he is a *very* striking character.
>
> Papa's appearance has been described many times, but very incorrectly. He has beautiful gray hair, not any too thick or any too long, but just right; a Roman nose, which greatly improves the beauty of his features; kind blue eyes and a small mustache. He has a wonderfully shaped head and profile. He has a very good figure—in short, he is an extraordinarily fine looking man. All his features are perfect, except that he hasn't extraordinary teeth. His complexion is very fair, and he doesn't ware [sic] a beard. He is a very good man and a very funny one. He

SAMUEL CLEMENS DOTED ON HIS DAUGHTERS: SUSY (LEFT), GOWNED FOR A CEREMONY AT BRYN MAWR COLLEGE IN 1890, AND CLARA, WHO WAS SIXTEEN THAT SAME YEAR.

has got a temper, but we all of us have in this family. He is the loveliest man I ever saw or ever hope to see—and oh, so absent-minded. He does tell perfectly delightful stories. Clara and I used to sit on each arm of his chair and listen while he told us stories about the pictures on the wall.

> — Susy Clemens, in her biography
> of her father

She did this work in her bedroom at night and kept her record hidden. After a little the mother discovered it and filched it and let me see it then told Susy what she had done and how pleased I was and how proud. . . . It is quite evident that several times, at breakfast and at dinner, in those long-past days, I was posing for the biography. In fact, I clearly remember that I *was* doing that—and I also remember that Susy detected it. I remember saying a very smart thing, with a good deal of an air, at the breakfast table one morning and that Susy observed to her mother privately a little later that papa was doing that for the biography.

> —Mark Twain

speaking tour. The tour was a success. He also started yet another business enterprise: a publishing company begun in partnership with his nephew Charley Webster.

Webster and Company published *The Adventures of Huckleberry Finn* in February 1885. Although it inspired a few favorable reviews from critics who liked Twain's use of language and his narrator, many rejected it for its critical view of society and religion.

Despite this criticism, the book did well. About 40,000 copies were sold in advance of its publication. Twain was also at work on another project that would be even more profitable. Former Union general and president Ulysses S. Grant had fallen on difficult times. Grant was bankrupt when Twain offered to help him write his memoirs. Webster and Company would publish it. Soon after, Grant developed cancer. He died before the two-volume *Personal Memoirs of U. S. Grant* was published in late 1885, but the phenomenal sales of the book brought almost a half-million dollars to his family, and more than $200,000 for Webster and Company.

Although the success of the book made Clemens wealthy, it was still not enough for him. Always looking for the next opportunity, Clemens met with James W. Paige, an inventor who had developed a plan for a machine that would set type much faster than men could do it by hand. If it worked as its inventor claimed, it would surely revolutionize both book and newspaper publishing. Between 1880 and 1885, Clemens invested $30,000 in Paige's invention, certain that it would soon bring him more wealth than he had ever imagined. Over the next few years, he would continue to pour more and more money into Paige's machine, even though Webster and Company had not had any major successes since Grant's memoirs.

Twain and "Culture"

"If you praise [Twain] among persons of Culture, they cannot believe that you are serious. They call him a Barbarian. They won't hear of him, they hurry from the subject; they pass by on the other side of the way. . . . But his art is not only that of a maker of the scarce article—mirth. I have no hesitation in saying that Mark Twain is one among the greatest of contemporary makers of fiction."

—Andrew Lang, *Illustrated London News*, 1891

By the end of 1887, Clemens had still seen no profit from the invention, but was continuing to invest in it. He began a new book, *A Connecticut Yankee in King Arthur's Court*. He hoped Paige's compositor would be perfected and ready to set the type for this book. Although the new book was ready in 1889, the compositor was not. With its nearly eighteen thousand parts, the machine was impossible to operate without it breaking down. Clemens continued to have faith in it, however. By the end of 1889, he had borrowed another $160,000 to invest.

The next year, 1890, brought even more trouble to the Clemens family. Both Samuel's and Livy's mothers died that year, and Clemens sank further in debt. Livy began having heart problems and her doctors suggested the Clemens' family travel to Europe for rest and medical treatment. Finally, at the beginning of 1891, Clemens had to quit making payments to Paige, although he still held interest in the invention. He continued to believe that the machine could work. He took the family overseas. The next two years were difficult ones. Webster and Company was losing money. Evidence suggested that a bookkeeper at Webster and Company had embezzled a great sum of

Samuel Clemens was always trying to "make a buck," over and above the money he earned by his writing and speaking tours. He poured a fortune into the Paige compositor, a machine that was meant to set type mechanically. If it had been successful, Clemens might indeed have become a very wealthy man; instead, he went into debt.

money, perhaps with the help of Clemens's nephew, Webster himself. In 1894, Twain released a new book on racial inequality, *The Tragedy of Pudd'nhead Wilson and the Comedy of Those Extraordinary Twins*, a novel in which the baby of a light-skinned slave woman was switched with the master's baby. The sales of the new book did little to improve the financial health of the Clemens family.

Clemens's financial troubles came to the attention of Henry Huttleston Rogers, co-founder and vice president of Standard Oil. Rogers was one of the wealthiest men in America, and he was also an admirer of Mark Twain's writing. Rogers offered his help as financial advisor. He hoped to save both the compositor and Webster and Company. In a working test of the Paige compositor, the machine broke down repeatedly and was clearly not suited to commercial use. Rogers finally convinced Clemens to give up on the compositor and declare bankruptcy. His inability to pay his debts was a hard blow to Clemens's pride.

Even during his troubles and his travel between Europe and the United States, Twain continued to write. He tried to capitalize on the popularity of his character Tom Sawyer with two new books: *Tom Sawyer Abroad* and *Tom Sawyer, Detective*. He also focused on a more serious subject. Since his youth he had been fascinated by the story of Joan of Arc, and he now turned that interest into a story entitled *Personal Recollections of Joan of Arc*. At first, it was published in monthly segments in *Harper's Magazine*. He did not allow his name to be attached to it because he believed that readers would not take it seriously knowing it came from the pen of the humorist Mark Twain. Later, it would be published as a book with his name on the cover. Susy admired it; many years later Twain would call it his favorite of all his books.

Twain on Twain

Many of Twain's words are still famous today. He enjoyed great popularity wherever he went, was often asked to speak at public affairs and private dinners, and was often quoted in newspapers. He was usually at his best when he made fun of himself and his own writing:

> "I shall not write poetry unless I conceive a spite against the subscribers."
> —1869 editorial from
> the *Buffalo Express*

> "I am not the editor of a newspaper, and shall always try to do right and be good, so that God will not make me one."
> —*Galaxy* magazine, 1870

> "Yes, high and fine literature is wine, and mine is only water. But everybody likes water."
> —Letter to W. D. Howells, 1887

> "I was sorry to have my name mentioned as one of the great authors because they have a sad habit of dying off. Chaucer is dead, Spenser is dead, so is Milton, so is Shakespeare, and I am not feeling very well myself."
> —speech before the Savage Club, London, 1899

Even though his bankruptcy meant that Clemens had no legal obligation to repay his debts, he worried about his honor. He was determined to pay back the money he had borrowed. Once again, he turned to the lecture stage to raise money. In 1895 he began a tour that included cities across the United States and around the world, almost 150 lectures in all.

Although Clemens would earn enough money to pay his creditors and regain his self-respect, the tour would carry far deeper personal costs for him.

Chapter 4

The Final Years

ONLY PART OF THE CLEMENS FAMILY embarked on the worldwide tour. Susy and Jean stayed with their aunt at Quarry Farm. Through July and August of 1895, Samuel, Livy, and Clara traveled by train to more than twenty cities across the United States and Canada. In the fall, they went overseas to Fiji, Australia, and New Zealand. They passed the winter in India, where Twain continued to perform for enthusiastic audiences. Next, they traveled to South Africa for the remainder of the tour. By the time they left South Africa in July 1896, Clemens had paid back about $35,000 toward his debts, and had a good start on a new book about his travels, *Following the Equator*.

Livy, Samuel, and Clara went to England. They sent a message to Susy and Jean, so the girls could travel to meet them there. A few days later they learned that Susy was too ill to travel. Livy and Clara boarded a ship for home, but before they arrived Susy, age twenty-four, had died of spinal meningitis. Clemens grieved for his daughter, and also for Livy and the girls who would have to learn of Susy's death without him to comfort them. Livy, Jean, and Clara made the funeral and burial arrangements; Clemens remained in England and blamed himself for the financial troubles that had caused his family to be separated. He seemed to believe that if they had been together, the outcome would have been different. According to biographer Paine, "[H]e now crucified himself as the slayer of Susy."

After the funeral, Livy, Jean, and Clara joined him in England, and the family moved to a new residence, telling

The Education of Helen Keller

In 1896, while the family was in London, Clemens learned of an extraordinary young American woman, Helen Keller, who had been deaf and blind since childhood. Despite these challenges, with the help of her teacher she had learned to speak and had proven herself capable of great learning. She had recently passed examinations to be admitted to Radcliffe College, but did not have the money to support herself and her teacher Anne Sullivan for the years of her education. Anne Sullivan needed to accompany her because of Keller's physical disabilities. Clemens considered writing to his friend Henry Huttleston Rogers, vice president of Standard Oil, to ask him to help finance the education of this young woman, but decided instead to approach Rogers's wife, saying, "Experience has convinced me that when one wished to set a hardworking man at something which he mightn't prefer to be bothered with it is best to move upon him behind his wife. If she can't convince him it isn't worth while for other people to try." Clemens was certain that, with a proper opportunity for education, Helen Keller "will make a fame that will endure for centuries." Rogers agreed to support Keller, and her teacher Anne Sullivan, throughout Keller's education.

only their closest friends the location. They grieved together, and did not celebrate Thanksgiving or Christmas that year. Twain turned to his work for release from grief and guilt. He readied *Following the Equator* for publication, revising it three times and accepting Livy's contribution of more than fifty pages of editorial notes. He continued to work on other projects as well, although most of his writings of this period of his life concentrated on the darker side of humanity and society. He wrote a story called "Which Was the Dream?" about a man who falls asleep and dreams that his house burns and his family dies. When he awakens, he cannot believe that the tragedy which was so real to him was only a dream, and instead believes that he is now only dreaming that his family lives.

Livy, the Editor

Ever since we have been married, I have been dependent on my wife to go over and revise my manuscript. . . . I can do the spelling and grammar alone—if I have a spelling book and a grammar with me—but I don't always know just where to draw the line in matters of taste. Mrs. Clemens has kept a lot of things from getting into print that might have given me a reputation I wouldn't care to have.

—Mark Twain

After a visit to Switzerland, the Clemens family moved to Vienna, Austria, in the winter of 1897–1898, so that Clara could study piano and voice with a famous teacher there. They enjoyed the social life of Vienna, but were not out of reach of grief. That December, Clemens received word that his brother Orion had died at the age of seventy-two.

Following the Equator was published in 1897, and sold 30,000 copies very quickly. The money from the book began to roll in, and Clemens instructed Rogers to put it toward the remaining debts. In January 1898, he finally paid off the last of his creditors with some money left over. The news made headlines in Europe and the United States. Clemens at last felt his honor was restored. Within a month, he had begun to invest in new money-making ventures, including a carpet-weaving machine.

The German Language

Through his many trips abroad, Twain often made fun of his attempts to speak other languages, especially German.

> I have not sufficiently mastered German to allow my using it with impunity. My collection of fourteen-syllable German words is still incomplete. But I have just added to that collection a jewel—a veritable jewel. I found it in a telegram from Linz, and it contains ninety-five letters:
>
> Personaleinkommensteuerschätzungskom missionsmitgliedreisekostenrechungsergän zungsrevisionsfund
>
> If I could get a similar word engraved upon my tombstone I should sleep beneath it in peace.
> —Mark Twain, 1899

In the summer of 1899, the Clemens family moved to a spa in Sweden to seek treatment from a doctor there for

A Remarkable Friendship

In 1869, William Dean Howells worked at the office of the popular magazine *The Atlantic Monthly*, as the assistant to the editor, James T. Fields. Howells often wrote reviews of recently published books, and that year he praised a new book, *Innocents Abroad*, by a relatively little-known author, Mark Twain. When Samuel Clemens arrived at Howell's office to thank him for his kind review, the two men began a friendship that would last over forty years.

Twain often sent Howells new manuscripts for his comments, and he accepted suggestions and criticisms from Howells more readily than from anyone else save Livy. Through the years, they exchanged hundreds of letters. After Clemens's death, Howells recalled, "Clemens . . . wrote with the greatest fullness and a lavish dramatization, sometimes to the length of twenty or forty pages, so that I have now perhaps fifteen hundred pages of his letters." At the conclusion of his introduction to *My Mark Twain*, Howells wrote, "He was a youth to the end of his days, the heart of a boy with the head of a sage; the heart of a good boy, or a bad boy, but always a willful boy, and wilfullest to show himself out at every time for just the boy he was."

Jean, who was suffering from increasingly frequent and serious epileptic seizures, a condition first diagnosed nine years earlier. That winter they followed the doctor to London to continue Jean's treatment. By the fall of 1900, they were homesick to return to the United States, and the doctor assured them they could find a doctor in New York who could continue Jean's therapy. Mark Twain the writer was as popular as ever, and Samuel Clemens was admired for his remarkable rise from bankruptcy.

Despite his celebrity, or perhaps because of it, the Clemens family was troubled. Jean was having frequent seizures and had to be watched constantly. According to Karen Lystra, professor of American Studies at California State University, Clara was enjoying the social life of New York, but Jean was often excluded because of her epilepsy. Jean's condition took a heavy emotional and physical toll on Livy. Livy and Samuel longed for the days when their children played happily around them. They could not stand the idea of returning to the house in Hartford where Susy had died. In 1901 they moved to Riverdale, New York. That autumn Clemens and his good friend William Dean Howells were honored with Doctorate of Letters degrees from Yale.

Mark Twain became more outspoken than ever in his criticism of politics, religion, war, and society. He spoke out against the imperialism that drove "civilized" countries to invade and conquer less developed nations in the name of freedom or religion, when, according to Twain, their real motive was greed. In December 1900, Twain wrote a welcome to the coming of the twentieth century that appeared in the *New York Herald*: "I bring you the stately matron named Christendom, returning bedraggled, besmirched, and dishonored from pirate raids in Kiao-Chou, Manchuria, South Africa, and the Philippines, with her soul full of meanness, her pocket full of boodle, and her mouth full of pious hypocrisies. Give her soap and a towel, but hide the looking-glass."

Some of his writings were so bitter that Livy asked him not to publish them during her lifetime. By this point in his life, he claimed that he cared more about his principles than he cared about the opinions of others or how his outspokenness would affect his income, but he still cared about Livy's feelings. In a letter to his longtime friend, Reverend Joseph Twichell, he wrote, "I am not expecting anything but kicks for scoffing, and am expecting a diminution of my bread and butter by it, but if Livy will let me, I will have my say." Despite this determination, however, Twain still enjoyed his popularity with the American people. He was continuously sought out by the press for his opinions on just about everything. Visitors came endlessly to the house. He made a trip to Hannibal in 1902, where he was celebrated and treated like royalty. The University of Missouri presented him with an honorary degree.

Some of Twain's writing was so strong in its criticism of society that he began a collection of works which he intended would not be published until after his death. "Only dead men can tell the truth in this world," he said. Outraged by the lynchings of blacks in the South, Twain wrote an essay entitled, "The United States of Lyncherdom." He even planned to publish a book on the subject, for which his essay would be the introduction. When he realized that it would completely alienate him from Southern readers, Twain changed his mind. He added it to the collection of manuscripts intended to be published after his death.

In 1902, Livy developed heart trouble. Concerned that her condition was caused by worry and overexcitement, her doctors allowed her husband to visit her sickroom only a few minutes a day. The next year, her doctors advised the family to travel to Italy for her health. She died in Florence on June 5, 1904. Samuel, Clara, and Jean returned to Elmira, New York, with Livy's body. Twain asked Reverend Twichell to officiate at the funeral, as he had at their wedding thirty-four years earlier.

On His Seventieth Birthday

"I have achieved my seventy years in the usual way: by sticking to a scheme of life which would kill anybody else. It sounds like an exaggeration, but that is really the common rule for attaining to old age. . . . I will offer here, as a sound maxim, this: That we can't reach old age by another man's road."
—Mark Twain

Soon after Livy's death, Clara suffered a nervous breakdown and committed herself to a sanitarium. Samuel and Jean moved to New York City, along with Katy Leary, their housekeeper of many years, and Isabelle Lyon, who worked as Samuel's personal assistant, handling the household business and taking dictation.

Words and Feelings

"Sometimes my feelings are so hot that I have to take the pen and put them out on paper to keep them from setting me afire inside; then all that ink and labor are wasted because I can't print the results."
—Mark Twain

He sent essays to magazines and also began working on his autobiography, some chapters of which were published in *The North American Review*. In 1906, he gave permission to a young man named Albert Bigelow Paine to write his official biography, and even invited Paine to move into the house, so they could work at all hours, with Clemens telling the stories of his life to Paine, as a stenographer wrote it all down. Lyon remained in the service of the Clemens family, and handled most of the household business, especially when Clara was not at home with the family. That same year, Clemens was invited to address Congress, to speak in favor of a bill enacting stricter copyright laws to protect authors. He also began a new fashion, dressing in white suits both winter and summer.

Mark Twain's white suits (adopted about 1906)

"But the white serge was an inspiration which few men would have had the courage to act upon. The first time I saw him wear it was at the authors' hearing before the Congressional Committee of Copyright in Washington. Nothing could have been more dramatic than the gesture with which he flung off his long loose overcoat, and stood forth in white from his feet to the crown of his silvery head. It was a magnificent coup, and he dearly loved a coup."

—W. D. Howells

To reporters gathered that day, Twain said:
"Why don't you ask why I am wearing such apparently unseasonable clothes? I'll tell you. I have found that when a man reaches the advanced age of seventy-one years, as I have, the continual sight of dark clothing is likely to have a depressing effect upon him. Light-colored clothing is more pleasing to the eye and enlivens the spirit. Now of course, I cannot compel every one to wear such clothing just for my especial benefit, so I do the next best thing and wear it myself."

Jean began to have seizures again, now more often than before. Clemens depended on Isabel Lyon to handle much of the care of his youngest daughter. Lyon's journals reveal that the secretary greatly admired her famous employer, but often felt burdened by the care Jean required. Jean sometimes resented Lyon's control over her freedom, and the two clashed. According to Karen Lystra's book, *Dangerous Intimacy*, Lyon succeeded in persuading Clemens to send Jean to a sanitarium for epileptics. Meanwhile, Clara was pursuing a singing career, and was seldom at home.

Twain was honored in 1907 by an invitation to return to England to receive an honorary doctorate degree from Oxford University. The Oxford degree was an amazing honor for a man who had only a few years of formal schooling in a small Missouri town. He was invited to Windsor Castle to visit the king and queen. He hired Ralph Ashcroft to work for him as a secretary and to be a traveling companion on the trip to England. During the trip, a rumor began circulating that Clemens and Lyon planned to marry. Clemens quickly dismissed the rumor, but he did not dismiss Lyon. After the trip to England, Lyon stayed on, managing the household affairs, including the budget, and Ashcroft continued to perform a variety of services for Clemens, including offering business advice. He was eventually named as Clemens's "business manager."

The Oxford Gown

"It is well known how proud he was of his Oxford gown, not merely because it symbolized the honor in which he was held by the highest literary body in the world, but because it was so rich and so beautiful. The red and the lavender of the cloth flattered his eyes as the silken black of the same degree of Doctor of Letters, given him years before at Yale, could not do. His frank, defiant happiness in it, mixed with a due sense of burlesque, was something that those lacking his poet-soul could never imagine; they counted it vain, weak; but that would not have mattered to him if he had known it."

—W. D. Howells

In 1908, Clemens moved into a new home in Redding, Connecticut. He called it Stormfield, after a character in a story he was writing. Upon settling at Stormfield, Clemens began to gather a new group of friends: young schoolgirls whom he would entertain at the house. According to Paine, Clemens was trying to replace the young family he missed so much from the Hartford days. "The years had robbed him of his own little flock," wrote Paine, "and always he was trying to replace them." Twain himself said, "I had reached the grandfather stage of life without grandchildren, so I began to adopt some." He named his little group "The Angelfish," and put up photos of colorful tropical fish on the walls of the billiards room. Each child chose a fish, and Clemens wrote her name on it. The girls and their mothers were invited to visit often at Stormfield.

Despite his welcome of the Angelfish to Stormfield, his own daughters seldom came. Lyon convinced Jean's doctor that Clemens did not want her to come to Stormfield, and she convinced Clemens that Jean was not well enough to come home. In the meantime, Clara was becoming worried about her father and the influence Lyon and Ashcroft appeared to have over him. In December 1908, she moved home to be with her father and investigate matters. In March 1909, Lyon and Ashcroft married. Clara was convinced that the two were taking advantage of her father, but could not prove it. In April, Isabel (Lyon) Ashcroft was dismissed from the household. Clara contacted Henry Rogers to look into her father's financial records. She also contacted Jean's doctor and arranged a meeting with her father. Jean was at last allowed to come to Stormfield. After an investigation, it was discovered that not only had Lyon managed to take money from Clemens for her own use, but she and Ashcroft had tricked Clemens into signing over to them complete legal authority over all his property, including Stormfield. Moreover, Ashcroft had convinced Clemens to invest $12,000 in several business enterprises of Ashcroft's, and over $50,000 in other companies in which Ashcroft had an interest.

Samuel Clemens modeled his last home, Stormfield, after the villas he and his family had lived in during their visit to Florence, Italy.

The Angelfish Club

Dorothy Quick met Samuel Clemens aboard the ocean liner *S. S. Minnetonka*, on the voyage from England to New York, after Twain had received his degree from Oxford. The two became good friends, and later, when the Angelfish Club was formed, Dorothy was invited to join.

> He told me all about the Aquarium Club, which he said "consists of a few very choice school-girl angel fishes and one slave. I am the slave." Then he pinned the glittering blue-green enamel angelfish on my dress and declared solemnly: "Dorothy Quick, you are now an angel fish—M.A.— which means 'Member of my Aquarium,' and I expect you to do it honor some day."

Dorothy and Samuel Clemens remained friends until his death, nearly three years later. As an adult, Quick became the author of many books. In her memoir, *Enchantment: A Little Girl's Friendship with Mark Twain*, she said,

> I don't know how the other Angelfish feel, but I am sure it must be the same with them as it is with me. For the time we knew him we lived in a rarefied atmosphere in which all things of life seemed to assume their true and proper proportions. We learned the simplicity of the great and the unassumption of the rich and true heart that held honor before everything and exalted right thinking and living to its highest degree.

"BE GOOD AND YOU WILL BE LONESOME" IS JUST ONE AMONG MANY LONG-LIVED QUOTES FROM THE CLASSIC HUMOROUS AUTHOR.

In 1909, Clemens continued to work every day at his writing, although he began to suffer from chest pains. He played billiards with Paine as he told him the stories of his life. Jean's condition had improved, and she was enthusiastically doing a great deal of hard work on the Stormfield property, and acting as her father's secretary. That October, Clara married Ossip Gabrilowitsch, a concert pianist. The ceremony took place on the lawn at Stormfield. The bride wore a white gown; her father wore his graduation robe and hat from the Oxford ceremony. Clara and Ossip left for Europe; Jean stayed at Stormfield to care for her father. On Christmas Eve, 1909, Jean suffered an epileptic seizure and drowned in the bathtub. Clemens was too weak to attend her funeral.

After Jean's death, Clemens decided to return once more to Bermuda. He enjoyed the tropical weather there, and the company of several of his Angelfish, who traveled with him. Within a few months, however, his health was failing. He returned to Stormfield in April of 1910. Clara and Ossip arrived to be at his side. On April 21, he slipped into a deep sleep and passed away.

igh the trees. I went for it, cautious and slow. By and
 close enough to have a look, and there laid a man on t
nd. It most give me the fantods. He had a blanket arou
head, and his head was nearly in the fire. I set the
 a clump of bushes in about six foot of him, and kept
on him steady. It was getting gray daylight now. Pret
he gapped and stretched himself and hove off the blank
t was Miss Watson's Jim! I bet I was glad to see him. I sa
o, Jim!" and skipped out.

unced up and stared at me wild. Then he drops down on
s, and puts his hands together and says:

Twain in Memorium

"Let us take leave of him here. The time is not one for
elaborate essays. He had the great human qualities.
Reading him, one came to love him as one loves Chaucer,
Fielding, and Ben Jonson. For all his war upon shams and
frauds, there was a vast benevolence in him, a genial tol-
erance, a deep human note. Truly a great man has gone
from among us."

—Anonymous, *Baltimore Sun*, 1910

truck? But you got a gun, hain't you? Den we kin git sum
r-den strawbries."

wberries and such truck," I says. "Is that what you li

uldn' git nuffn else," he says.

 how long you been on the island, Jim?"
me heah de night arter you's killed."
t, all that time?"
-- indeedy."
ain't you had nothing but that kind of rubbage to eat?
sah -- nuffn else."
, you must be most starved, ain't you?"
ck'n I could eat a hoss. I think I could. How long you b
e islan'?"
e the night I got killed."
by and by, sure enough, I catched a glimpse of fire aw
ugh the trees. I went for it, cautious and slow. By and
s close enough to have a look, and there laid a man on t
nd. It most give me the fantods. He had a blanket arou

hat, all that time?"

es -- indeedy."

nd ain't you had nothing but that kind of rubbage to e

o, sah -- nuffn else."

ell, you must be most starved, ain't you?"

reck'n I could eat a hoss. I think I could. How long yo

ince the night I got killed."

t by and by, sure enough, I catched a glimpse of fire a

was close enough to have a look, and there laid a man o

is head, and his head was nearly in the fire. I set the

yes on him steady. It was getting gray daylight now. P

et, and it was Miss Watson's Jim! I bet I was glad to see

ello, Jim!" and skipped out.

e bounced up and stared at me wild. Then he drops down

oan' hurt me -- don t! I hain't ever done no harm to a g

n git in de river agin, whah you b'longs, en doan' do nu

ell, I warn't long making him understand I warn't dead.

arn't afraid of HIM telling the people where I was. I tal

ng. Then I says:

t's good daylight. Le's get breakfast. Make up your camp

hat's de use er makin' up de camp fire to cook strawbries

etter den strawbries."

trawberries and such truck," I says. "Is that what you

couldn' git nuffn else," he says.

hy, how long you been on the island, Jim?"

come heah de night arter you's killed."

hat, all that time?"

es -- indeedy."

nd ain't you had nothing but that kind of rubbage to e

o, sah -- nuffn else."

ell, you must be most starved, ain't you?"

reck'n I could eat a hoss. I think I could. How long yo

ince the night I got killed."

t by and by, sure enough, I catched a glimpse of fire a

was close enough to have a look, and there laid a man o

is head, and his head was nearly in the fire. I set the

yes on him steady. It was getting gray daylight now. Pr

et, and it was Miss Watson's Jim! I bet I was glad to see

ello, Jim!" and skipped out.

e bounced up and stared at me wild. Then he drops down

oan' hurt me -- don t! I hain't ever done no harm to a gr

n git in de river agin, whah you b'longs, en doan' do nu

ell, I warn't long making him understand I warn't dead.

de islan'?"

gh the trees. I went for it, cautious and slow. By and b
nd. It most give me the fantods. He had a blanket aroun
a clump of bushes in about six foot of him, and kept m
he gapped and stretched himself and hove off the bla
ys:

ees, and puts his hands together and says:
vuz liked dead people, en done all I could for 'em. You g
e Jim, 'at 'uz awluz yo' fren'."
er so glad to see Jim. I warn't lonesome now. I told him
, but he only set there and looked at me; never said not
d."
ruck?
we kin git sumf

Part II:
A Reader's Guide to
The Adventures of
Huckleberry Finn

de islan'?"

gh the trees, I went for it, cautious and slow. By and b
nd. It most give me the fantods. He had a blanket aroun
a clump of bushes in about six foot of him, and kept n
he gapped and stretched himself and hove off the bla
ays:

nees, and puts his hands together and says:
vuz liked dead people, en done all I could for 'em. You g
le Jim, 'at 'uz awluz yo' fren'."
er so glad to see Jim. I warn't lonesome now. I told him

was close enough to have a look, and there laid a man o
ound. It most give me the fantods. He had a blanket a
s head; and his head was nearly in the fire. I set
nind a clump of bushes in about six foot of him, and ke
es on him steady. It was getting gray daylight now. P
n he ga
d it wa
llo, Ji
bounce
ees, an
an' hur
wuz lik
in de
n, 'at 'u
ll, I wa
er so g
rn't af
ong, bu
. Then
's good
d."
at's de
h truc
ter de
rawbe
"
couldn'
y, how
come he
at, all
s -- in
d ain't
, sah -
ll, you
reck'n I could eat a hoss. I think I could. How long you
de islan'?"
nce the night I got killed."
t by and by, sure enough, I catched a glimpse of fire
rough the trees. I went for it, cautious and slow. By an
was close enough to have a look, and there laid a man on
ound. It most give me the fantods. He had a blanket and
s head, and his head was nearly in the fire. I set

Adventures of HUCKLEBERRY Finn.

(Tom Sawyer's Comrade.)

BY

MARK TWAIN.

ILLUSTRATED.

THE ADVENTURES OF HUCKLEBERRY FINN WAS ORIGINALLY MARKETED AS A COMPANION TO TOM SAWYER, A MUCH-LESS-COMPLICATED BOYS' ADVENTURE STORY.

Chapter 1

Examining *The Adventures of Huckleberry Finn*

THE ADVENTURES OF HUCKLEBERRY FINN is probably Twain's most well-known book. Millions of Americans have read the book—many because it was required by their school's curriculum. Today, the novel is required reading in fewer schools, but it is still considered a classic of American literature and is read worldwide. When he finished the draft of the story in 1883, Twain could not have predicted that his book would be so famous for so long. He did, however, guess that it would cause controversy. When he was almost done, he wrote to his friend William Dean Howells, saying, "And I shall like it, whether anybody else does or not."

Twain begins the book with a mock threatening notice: "Persons attempting to find a motive in this narrative will be prosecuted; persons attempting to find a moral in it will be banished; persons attempting to find a plot in it will be shot." Regardless of this threat, readers wanting to fully understand the story must look at all three.

A Masterpiece

"What is it we want in a novel? We want a vivid and original picture of life; we want character naturally displayed in action, and if we get the excitement of adventure into the bargain, and that adventure possible and plausible, I so far differ from the newest school of criticism as to think that we have additional cause for gratitude. If, moreover, there is an unstrained sense of humour in the narrator, we have a masterpiece and *Huckleberry Finn* is nothing less."
—Andrew Lang, 1891

The Plot

The Adventures of Huckleberry Finn is often classified as a picaresque novel; that is, a story about a clever rascal involved in a series of adventurous episodes. In fact, there are many rascals and rogues in the book, and their adventures show the reader as much about pre-Civil War American life and culture in small towns along the Mississippi as they do about the characters themselves.

The beginning of *The Adventures of Huckleberry Finn* leads the reader to believe that this book is intended as a continuation of *The Adventures of Tom Sawyer*. Huck introduces himself to the reader by referring to that earlier book. The story picks up from the ending of *Tom Sawyer*, with Tom and Huck among the wealthiest citizens of the town due to their discovery of the treasure from Injun Joe's cave. Because Huck's only parent, Pap, has been missing for some time, Huck lives with the Widow Douglas, who is trying to "civilize" him by insisting that he attend school, go to church, and wear clean clothes. Through Huck's simple voice, the reader is able to understand this boy. He wants to please the widow, but still enjoys having adventures with Tom and the gang. The first few chapters contain the same type of humor and mischief that made Tom Sawyer popular, including Tom's imaginative use of stories of genies, robbers, and pirates in their play.

By the beginning of Chapter Four, Huck is growing comfortable in his new life. However, when Pap returns to lay claim to Huck's fortune, the story takes a much more serious tone. Although Twain includes some humor when a well-meaning judge tries to reform Pap, the general mood of the book takes a dark turn. The reader is soon sympathetic to Huck's situation when the boy is kidnapped and abused by his alcoholic father. By the end of Chapter Seven, Huck has combined Tom Sawyer's love of

A SCENE FROM *TOM SAWYER*, THE BOOK THAT PRECEDED *HUCKLEBERRY FINN*.

theatrics with his own need to escape, and has managed to fake his own murder. He sets up camp on an island in the Mississippi River, and plans to begin a new life on his own, far away from St. Petersburg, Missouri.

Chapters Eight through Eleven begin the next part of Huck's story: his plans are complicated by the discovery of Miss Watson's slave, Jim, who has escaped and is also hiding on Jackson's Island. They spend a few days on the island, enjoying their freedom and getting to know each other. They paddle their canoe out to investigate a house that comes floating down the river. Inside, they find a dead man, but Jim covers him so that Huck cannot see him. They begin to wonder what is going on in St. Petersburg, and Huck disguises himself as a girl and returns to St. Petersburg, where he meets Judith Loftus. She has recently moved to town, and so does not know Huck, although she quickly realizes he is not really a girl. She also knows all about the town gossip, including Huck's murder and Jim's escape. She tells him that Jim is suspected of Huck's murder and some men are planning to go to Jackson's Island to look for him. Huck hurries back to warn Jim, and they outfit a raft and begin their adventures on the river.

Twain uses Chapters Twelve through Sixteen to further develop the characters of both Jim and Huck. At times they are alone on the raft, and they talk and get to know each other better. Still, they are not free of the influence of society. They come upon a partly sunken boat and decide to land on it for some Tom Sawyer-style adventure. They soon find out that they are not alone: three thieves are on the boat, and have filled a skiff with loot. Huck overhears their conversation and learns that two of the thieves plan to leave their companion on the boat to drown. He and Jim then discover that their raft has broken loose. Their only escape is to take the thieves' skiff, leaving the three men on the sinking boat. Huck alerts the captain of a ferry-boat that someone is stuck on the sinking boat, but by that time, there is no chance that anyone is still alive on it. Huck and Jim plan to watch for the lower tip of Illinois, where the Ohio River flows into the Mississippi. There they plan to go ashore on the Illinois side, sell the raft, and travel on a riverboat up the Ohio River to the free states where Jim can escape slavery. As they get closer, Jim makes plans for his future, and Huck becomes more worried about his role in "stealing" Jim. Eventually, they discover that they have passed the mouth of the Ohio River in a fog, and so lost Jim's chance for freedom. Then, a steamboat crashes into the raft and separates Huck and Jim as they swim for their lives.

Huck makes it to shore near a big log cabin, the home of the Grangerfords. He is impressed by their wealth and refinement. The Grangerfords are kind to Huck. When he explains his situation by telling them he is an orphan, they even offer to let him stay as long as he wants. He makes friends with young Buck Grangerford, who is about his age. Huck soon discovers that the Grangerfords and their neighbors, the Shepherdsons, are involved in a feud. After a gunfight in which Buck is killed, Huck runs away and meets up again with Jim, who has been hidden in the woods by some of the Grangerfords' slaves. Jim has fixed the raft and collected supplies for them, and they begin the next part of their journey.

Although they hope to regain the peacefulness of their earlier time together on the raft, they soon find themselves in the company of two con men who both claim to be the lost heirs of European royalty. Huck soon recognizes the "rapscallions" for what they are, but Twain uses their adventures in Chapters Nineteen through Thirty-one to paint a portrait of life in the South in which ordinary citizens are easy prey of con men, and there is no honor even among thieves. Their scams include a moving testimony in which one claims to be a pirate "reformed" by a traveling preacher at a camp-meeting, a Shakespearean play which is later degraded to a naked romp on stage, and even pretending to be the long-lost brothers of a wealthy man who has recently passed away. For the most part, Huck is not involved in these schemes, and merely describes them for the reader. When he must play a role in the plan to cheat the Wilks girls of their uncle's money, however, he cannot continue the act, and makes a plan to have the duke and king caught in their scam. At last Huck thinks he and Jim might be free of the two con men. Instead, the men manage to escape and, desperate for cash, they give Jim over to the custody of a local farmer in exchange for forty dollars. Huck now truly mourns the loss of his friend. Although he considers writing home to Jim's owner in order to clear his own conscience, he finally decides that he must steal Jim out of slavery, and so condemn himself to hell.

The final section of the book tells the story of Huck's attempt to free Jim. Although the reader expects this to be very serious business, the mood changes very quickly. Huck tracks Jim down to the farm owned by Sally and Silas Phelps. When he gets there, Huck is surprised that Sally Phelps seems to know him. He soon finds out that the Phelpses are Tom Sawyer's aunt and uncle, and Aunt Sally thinks Huck is Tom, whom she is expecting for a visit. When Tom arrives, Huck must tell him all, including his plan to free Jim. Huck is amazed when Tom, despite his "respectable upbringing," agrees to help. In typical Tom Sawyer style, Tom hatches an elaborate plan that includes baking a rope ladder in a giant pie, digging a tunnel into a shed, taming rats and spiders as "pets" for Jim, and forcing the illiterate slave to keep a journal written with his own blood. The climax of the episode is a daring escape attempt in which Tom is shot and Jim is

SAM CLEMENS AND HIS FRIEND AND COMPANION AT QUARLES FARM, JOHN T. LEWIS, THOUGHT TO HAVE INFLUENCED HIS PORTRAYAL OF JIM IN *THE ADVENTURES OF HUCKLEBERRY FINN*.

returned to the Phelps's farm after he helps the doctor care for Tom. In the resolution of the story, Tom's Aunt Polly arrives to expose the boys' masquerade, and Tom reveals the fact that Jim was actually freed by his owner, Miss Watson, two months before. Jim then tells Huck that Pap is also dead, and Huck ends his story with his plan to go West to the territories, because "Aunt Sally she's going to adopt me and sivilize me and I can't stand it. I been there before."

Twain's Reason for Writing the Novel

Twain's motive for writing *Huck Finn* is not quite so simple, and may have changed as the book progressed. To better understand this, it helps to examine events in Twain's life as he worked on it. He began the story of Huckleberry Finn in 1876, during his annual summer visit to Quarry Farm. He had recently finished *Tom Sawyer*, and began the story as a sequel to that book. He still had a great deal of descriptive material from his boyhood that he had not yet used, and he now had the opportunity to step outside his own viewpoint (or that of Tom Sawyer), and look through the eyes of a different character. This story would be told by Huck himself, with his own simple and uneducated view of religion and life in St. Petersburg and the Widow Douglas's efforts to civilize him. It also included more development of the slave Jim, patterned after a slave named Uncle Dan'l whom Clemens had known on his uncle's farm. At this point, Twain's motive seemed to be the desire to produce another lighthearted boy's book that incorporated humor and scenes from his own boyhood.

By the end of the summer, however, Twain seemed to be having difficulty with the book. In a letter to William Dean Howells on August 9, he wrote, "I . . . began another boy's book—more to be at work than anything else. I have written 400 pages on it—therefore it is very nearly half done. It is Huck Finn's Autobiography. I like it only tolerably well, as far as I have got, & may possibly pigeonhole it or burn the MS when it is done." Scholars who have studied the manuscript believe that Twain probably wrote most of the first sixteen chapters of the book that summer, except for Chapters Twelve and Thirteen, concerning the wreck of the *Walter Scott*, which were probably added to the manuscript in 1883. This would take Huck out of St. Petersburg and down the Mississippi with Jim to the point where the raft was smashed by the riverboat near the Grangerford's farm. The manuscript was apparently set aside for several years.

The years 1876 to 1879 were busy ones for the Clemens family and for Mark Twain the writer. Clemens participated in politics during the presidential election campaign of Rutherford Hayes in 1876. *The Adventures of Tom Sawyer* was published in December of that year. Twain worked on plays during that winter and the following summer. In spring of 1878, the family went abroad to Europe for nearly eighteen months. While abroad, Twain struggled with his new travel book, *A Tramp Abroad*, destroying more pages than he kept. He did not finish it until after the family returned to the United States in fall of 1879.

Twain may have simply had too many other projects and concerns to think about Huck's story. Despite these commitments, it appears that Twain did return at least briefly to the unfinished manuscript. According to notes he made, he probably wrote the Grangerford section of the book, Chapters Seventeen and Eighteen, during the winter of 1879–1880. Livy was pregnant that winter, and Samuel was concerned about her health. Daughter Jean was born in July 1880. He set the manuscript aside for several more years.

Of Paper and Pens: Walter Blair's Detective Work

Many details about Twain's work in the writing of *The Adventures of Huckleberry Finn* come from the research of Walter Blair. During the 1940s and 1950s, Blair conducted a study of Twain's writing by examining surviving notebooks, letters, journals, and manuscripts that could be dated between 1876 and 1884. He went to many libraries where the papers were kept and wrote to still other libraries to which he could not travel. He studied the types of paper, colors of ink, and other characteristics of the notes, in order to discover when and where Twain wrote the different parts of *Huckleberry Finn*. Blair recalled, "I had a memorable experience—spending hours, not reading Twain's words, but noticing the kind of writing material used and holding up pages to the light so that I might discover watermarks in thousands of pages." His findings from his research sound a little bit like clues from a Sherlock Holmes detective story:

> Although [Twain] wrote in pencil at random, when he wrote with ink he used violet ink consistently between these dates: late November, 1876, and mid-June, 1877; late September, 1877, and late March, 1878; mid-November, 1879, and mid-June, 1880. He used it sporadically in Europe during the winter of 1878–79. Therefore, except when abroad, he used such ink only in Hartford. Every time he went to Quarry Farm he switched to black, bluish-gray, or brown ink or to pencil; then, soon after returning to Hartford, he began to use violet again.

This detailed research helped Blair determine that Twain wrote the Grangerford section of the book during 1879–80, although earlier scholars had believed that Twain did not work on the book between the summer of 1876 when he began it at Quarry Farm, and the summer of 1883, when he finished the first draft there. Blair also makes convincing connections between parts of the story and important events in Clemens's life, as well as the reading he did during this period.

Twain was also working on a new book, *The Prince and the Pauper*. On his Continental trip in 1878–1879, he began to lose some of the admiration he had previously held for Europeans. As he learned more history, the monarchy of England now seemed less noble than he had thought previously. His notes contained mention of cruelties such as "Religious burnings . . . 60,000 in prison for debt and crime . . . 72,000 executed in Henry's reign, for theft and robbery. Drunken habits of James I and his court . . . " and others. Some of this dislike for European nobility can certainly be seen in *Huckleberry Finn* in the characters of the Duke and Dauphin, scoundrels who pretend to be descended from European royalty.

While he was certainly busy with his family and his other writing projects, Twain may also have been having difficulty with the story of Huck and Jim that kept him from progressing with it. Once Huck and Jim passed the mouth of the Ohio River (Chapter Fifteen), they could only progress further into the slave states of the South. The danger for a runaway slave would increase as they continued on their journey. Also, the Grangerford/Shepherdson feud which ended in the killing of Huck's new friend, Buck Grangerford, added a new dimension of tragedy to the story. Perhaps this book was not a "boy's story" after all.

In 1882, Twain took a steamboat trip down the Mississippi to gather material to finish his book *Life on the Mississippi*. The South had changed a great deal in the years since the Civil War, but freed slaves were still denied status as full citizens throughout many areas of the South. Many white people remembered the days of slavery fondly, associating it with wealth and prosperity instead of with the savage cruelty that was the reality of life for slaves. Freed slaves were also victimized by mobs of whites as well as by the more organized Ku Klux Klan. Reports of lynchings, shootings, and other violence against African Americans in southern states circulated throughout the country. Critic Peter Messent notes that, according to

Twain scholar Shelley Fisher Fishkin, Twain began collecting newspaper clippings as early as the 1870s about Klan violence and other brutality against African Americans in the South.

Huck's story was now much more than the simple and humorous story of boyhood adventure in *Tom Sawyer*. Like Samuel Clemens, Huck grew up in a society that accepted slavery and the idea of human beings as property. In his autobiography Twain wrote, "In my schoolboy days I had no aversion to slavery. I was not aware that there was anything wrong about it. No one arraigned it in my hearing; the local papers said nothing against it; the local pulpit taught us that God approved it." Despite the outcome of the Civil War, many people still held these beliefs. Clemens himself, however, had changed his mind about it. Critic Neil Schmitz believes that in 1883 the author was dealing with the personal conflict of facing his own role as a soldier in, and a deserter from, the militia unit which was formed to fight against Union troops.

While the very public Mark Twain was attending banquets in the North and making toasts to Union generals like the late Ulysses S. Grant, he had his own past to deal with. Schmitz describes Twain as "the Southern humorist gone over, not just a deserter, a dissenter, but a literary scalawag, a Southern writer in Unionist discourse and narrative." Clemens now felt very strongly against slavery, but he seemed to sometimes feel the need to make up for his acceptance of it in his early years. William Dean Howells described his friend as "the most desouthernized Southerner I ever knew. No man more perfectly sensed and more entirely abhorred slavery. . . . He held himself responsible for the wrong which the white race had done the black race in slavery." Schmitz says that "*Huckleberry Finn* is not only about running away, it is also about the fright and guilt in changing sides."

The outcome of *Huckleberry Finn* was now clear: The simple and honest Huck must reject the moral teachings of his society and even his religion as he accepts the humanity of his friend, Jim. Now that he knew his motive, Twain could finish the book. He added the sinking of the wrecked steamboat *Walter Scott* to the earlier part of the novel and continued Huck and Jim's journey down the Mississippi. By the end of the summer of 1883, Twain had drafted the rest of *The Adventures of Huckleberry Finn*, although he continued to ask advice of Howells and made changes to the manuscript during the coming months.

Literature Hooked on Sunday

When he returned to writing *Huckleberry Finn* in the summer of 1883, Twain was finally enjoying it. He was also more productive than he had been in quite some time. Near the end of the summer he wrote to Howells about his summer of writing:

> I've done two seasons' work in one, & haven't anything left to do, now, but revise. I've written eight or nine hundred MS pages in such a brief space of time that I mustn't name the number of days; I shouldn't believe it myself, & of course couldn't expect you to. I used to restrict myself to 4 & 5 hours a day & 5 days in the week; but this time I've wrought from breakfast until 5:15 p.m. six days a week; and once or twice I smouched a Sunday when the boss wasn't looking. Nothing is half so good as literature hooked on Sunday on the sly.

The Moral of the Story

Determining the "moral" or message of *Huckleberry Finn* is not as easy as it may seem. Although the main message of the book concerns slavery, Twain worked many ideas

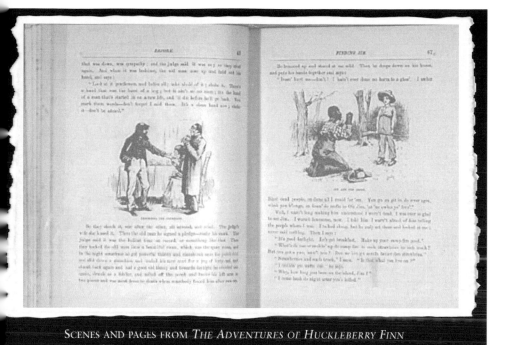

SCENES AND PAGES FROM *THE ADVENTURES OF HUCKLEBERRY FINN*

together, including the hypocrisy of religion, individual morality, and the cruelty and violence hidden behind the mask of gentility in Southern aristocracy. These ideas are so closely tied together that it is difficult to discuss them separately. One way to approach Twain's message is through the examination of characters in the book.

Probably the easiest character to discuss is Jim. Twain patterned Jim after a middle-aged slave on the Quarles farm, Uncle Dan'l, whom he described as "a faithful and affectionate good friend, ally, and advisor." He admitted, "I have not seen him for more than half a century, and yet spiritually I have had his welcome company a good part of the time, and have staged him in books under his own name and as 'Jim' . . . and he endured it with all the patience and friendliness and loyalty which were his birthright."

Jim is the most moral character in *The Adventures of Huckleberry Finn*. He is kind and loving to Huck, worries about him when he thinks Huck is in trouble, and rejoices when they are reunited. He becomes the kind of father figure the boy has never had. Before the Civil War, slave-holders justified their treatment of their human property by insisting that blacks were no more than animals that didn't care about their families. They also characterized them as ignorant, violent, and inhuman. Jim breaks down all these stereotypes. He ran away because Miss Watson wanted to sell him away from his family. He cries at night because he misses his wife and children, and he feels guilty about the way he treated his little daughter before he discovered she was deaf. His fondest dream is to free himself, then earn enough money to buy his wife and children out of slavery.

Jim's superstitions are those that young Samuel remembered from his summers at the Quarles farm, and they are mostly harmless, having to do with dream interpretation, sickness, good luck and bad, and evil spirits. The only time Jim lies is when he tells the tale about being "ridden by witches" in Chapter Two, and on that occasion, Jim appears to have convinced himself that this story was true. Jim is also honest with his friend Huck. When Huck tries to trick him into thinking that the fog near Cairo had all been a dream, Jim tells Huck what he thinks about it, "Dat truck dah is trash, en trash is what people is dat puts dirt on de head or dey fren's en makes 'em ashamed." Despite the misery inflicted upon him by the Duke and King, Jim continues to display patience and trust that Huck will be true to his word and not turn him in. He endures the indignity of the Duke's plan to keep him tied up while on the raft, being painted blue and labeled a "sick Arab," and the discomfort of his captivity during Tom's elaborate plan to free him. He even sacrifices his own freedom to help the doctor care for Tom.

Completely opposite of Jim is the worst character of the book: Pap Finn. Pap is both greedy and violent. Pap is willing to let the Judge "reform" him so that he can gain custody of Huck and get his money. He clearly only cares about his son when he thinks he can take his money. Pap is uneducated, dirty, often drunk, and always looked down upon, but he manages to take pride in those characteristics. He berates Huck because the boy learns to read, prays, and wears clean clothes. Pap believes that he deserves both respect and his son's riches. When he rants about a light-skinned, educated Negro being able to vote, his main complaint is that even that black man gets more respect than he does from the "gov'mint." He beats Huck without remorse and, in his "delirium tremens," even threatens his life. Ultimately, the reader is satisfied that Pap's murder was exactly what he deserved. When Jim tells Huck that Pap is dead, Huck shows no emotional reaction at all, neither sadness nor relief.

Both Huck and Twain seem to feel a little more sympathetic toward the other scoundrels of the novel, the Duke and the Dauphin. These two are greedy and willing to cheat anyone to increase their own wealth. They especially like to prey upon the kindness of others. The Dauphin pretends to be a converted pirate at a religious camp-meeting to get money from the religious people in town. The Duke and Dauphin intend to cheat the Wilks girls of their inheritance and property. Despite their greed, however, the Duke and the Dauphin are not violent. The people they cheat give them their money willingly. This is as true of the people at the camp-meeting as it is of those who buy tickets to the Royal Nonesuch, drawn by its advertisement, "Ladies and Children Not Admitted." Even the Wilks girls willingly give the men their money.

The Duke and the Dauphin may be rapscallions of the first order, but they accept themselves for what they are. They do not deceive themselves into thinking they are good and moral people. They know they are scoundrels, and they are not sorry about it. They may pretend otherwise in order to convince someone else they deserve consideration, but they never really fool themselves. When they first meet in Chapter Nineteen, the Duke and the Dauphin share their past scams as if they were job resumés. Later, when they make a narrow escape from the Wilks episode, they immediately set to work planning their next series of scams. Huck tells us, "They tackled missionarying, and mesmerizing, and doctoring, and telling fortunes, and a little of everything; but they couldn't seem to have no luck."

Huck does not like to be mixed up with these con men. He is glad when he thinks they have been left behind at the Wilks grave, and nearly cries when he sees them rowing toward the raft on a skiff. Soon afterward, they commit their worst crime from Huck's viewpoint, using the phony runaway slave handbill to trade Jim for forty dollars. Despite their crimes, however, Huck is sympathetic toward them when he sees them tarred and feathered. From the reader's viewpoint, these characters deserve their punishment, but when Huck finds out from Uncle Silas what the townspeople have planned for them, he attempts to warn them. Why does Twain let Huck feel sympathy toward them? Perhaps because he saves the worst punishment for hypocrites.

The Grangerford family presents the reader with a view of pre-Civil War slaveholding Southern aristocracy. The family is kind to Huck, who tells us that "Col. Grangerford . . . was a gentleman all over." Huck is impressed that they "owned a lot of farms, and over a hundred niggers." Each member of the family has his own slave, and even young Buck makes sure that his has plenty to do. Through Huck's unsophisticated eyes, the Grangerfords are the very essence of Southern nobility, from their cuckoo clock that "would start in and strike a hundred and fifty before she got tuckered out" to their elaborate brandy toast to their parents each morning. Still, the reader can soon see that this outward image is as false as the fruit in the crockery bowl on the table that was "prettier than real ones is, but they warn't real because you could see where pieces had got chipped off and showed the white chalk . . . underneath."

The family has long been engaged in a feud with their neighbors the Shepherdsons. They sit through church together listening to a sermon on brotherly love with their guns propped against the wall. The Colonel insists on "honorable" behavior in the feud, and scolds Buck about shooting from behind a bush. Buck's account of the feud sounds like a cross between a twisted weather forecast—"Right smart chance of funerals"—and a score card—"We got one and they got one."

The only Grangerford who seemed to understand the tragedy of the situation was their deceased young daughter, Emmeline, who wrote poetry based on obituaries, and drew pictures of tombstones. Through Emmeline's poetry and artwork, Twain mocks the English "graveyard school" of poetry, and the preoccupation of the Southern aristocracy with British literature. Although Emmeline's overly sentimental verses are about people she did not know, the reader at least senses in her a soul too sensitive to survive in the midst of this violence. Huck is so moved by the dead girl's poetry that he even tries to "sweat out a verse or two" himself. Ultimately, the Grangerford/Shepherdson feud erupts in barbaric violence. By the end of the episode at least seven men and boys are dead. In the strongest emotion he has expressed so far, Huck recognizes the useless loss of life and mourns his friend. He tells us he cried as he covered up Buck's face and admits, "I wished I hadn't ever come ashore that night, to see such things."

As Huck and Jim continue their journey, they come into contact with many nameless people on the river and in small towns who have relatively minor roles in the story. These common people are usually concerned only with their own welfare, such as the men Huck speaks to on the river who, rather than risk smallpox to help this boy in apparently grave circumstances, give him money; or the robbers on the sinking boat who are about to murder their partner.

In "Pokeville" the townspeople are gullible enough to believe that a pirate has come into their small town, been saved at the camp meeting, and is now committed to going back to the seas as a missionary to convert other pirates. In Bricksville, the people are ignorant and low-minded. They are easy prey for the Royal Nonesuch. One of the most violent scenes of the book takes place in Bricksville. An unarmed, drunken man is shot down in the street by a man whom he has insulted. When the crowd turns into an angry lynch mob, the killer, Colonel Sherburn, turns on them with this speech:

> The average man's a coward ... the average man don't like trouble and danger. *You* don't like trouble and danger. But if only *half* a man—like Buck Harkness there—shouts 'Lynch him, lynch him!' you're afraid to back down—afraid you'll be found out for what you are—*cowards*. ... If any real lynching's going to be done, it will be done in the dark, Southern fashion, and when they come they'll bring their masks, and fetch a *man* along.

The neighbors of the deceased Peter Wilks and his nieces are just as gullible as the Bricksville crowd. They fall for the phony English accent of the Dauphin and the Duke's crazy sign language. When the real brothers of Peter Wilks show up, however, the townspeople form a mob just as quickly as the Bricksville crowd. The only thing that saves Huck and the scoundrels is the greedy nature of the mob. When they discover the bag of gold in the coffin, they all let go of their prisoners to get a better look at it. Through these scenes, Twain paints a grim portrait of Southern society.

"Mark Twain told America, 'This is how you are, like it or not.'"

—teacher Margaret Norris, 2000

Some characters in the book stand out from the regular crowd, though. These characters are good people, but have been misguided by their society and religious leaders. They are kind to Huck despite his background, and are concerned about his welfare, although they are not interested in his money. They believe that slavery is acceptable, but still do not like to see slaves mistreated. Both the widow and Miss Watson fit this description. The widow is more kind to Huck and concerned about his welfare, but even Miss Watson seems to want to improve Huck to make a better person of him. Although Miss Watson is tempted by the slave-trader's offer of eight hundred dollars for Jim, on her deathbed she feels guilty for her greed and sets him free.

The Wilks girls also are basically good people. Mary Jane scolds her sister for questioning Huck's stories about England, and mourns for the slaves whom her "uncles" sold away from their families. When Huck tells her the truth, she is happy to find out that the slaves will be returned, and forgives Huck for his part in the scam.

Uncle Silas and Aunt Sally are also basically good-hearted, even though they paid forty dollars for Jim in the hopes of collecting a two hundred dollar reward. They too, really care about Huck, and even want to adopt him. Their treatment of Jim is despicable by modern standards of human rights and dignity, but compared with pre-Civil

War standards of treatment for slaves in the South, especially slaves suspected of being runaways, it is fairly mild. Although they confine Jim in a small shed, they send generous plates of food out to him. His leg is shackled to the bed, but the end of the chain is merely slipped around the leg of the bed, and could easily be freed by just lifting it up. The shed is not guarded, and the slave who brings Jim's dinner carries the key to the padlock. Jim could easily escape if he really wanted to, and any of the other slaves could have helped him do so.

Perhaps Twain allows the reader to like these characters because he was himself raised in this culture and accepted these views. If we accept that Tom Sawyer was in fact modeled after Samuel Clemens, then we can sense Huck's disappointment that Tom would help with the plan to free Jim, an action that was morally wrong in Southern society and punishable under laws that carried severe penalties for helping a runaway slave.

The only major character left to discuss is Huckleberry himself. Twain said that he patterned Huck after Tom Blankenship, the son of the town drunk in Hannibal. According to Twain's autobiography, "He was ignorant, unwashed, insufficiently fed; but he had as good a heart as ever any boy had. . . . He was the only really independent person—boy or man in the community, and by consequence he was tranquilly and continuously happy and was envied by all the rest of us."

Huck is different from other characters in the book because his father's outcast status has led to Huck's separation from the mainstream of society for his whole life. Therefore, the "rules" of society are new to him, and are about as uncomfortable as the new clothes the widow puts on him. He would prefer to go barefoot, sleep outdoors, and spit whenever he felt like it. Still, the widow's kindness and patience help him slowly become accustomed to civilized life and customs. He learns about religion and acquires a conscience, and that's where the trouble begins for him. Throughout the rest of the book, his new sense of morality causes him trouble.

When Huck discovers Jim hiding on Jackson's Island, he is faced with a dilemma. Huck knows he must escape in order to be free of Pap. Jim also needs to escape to avoid being sold down the river away from his family. If Huck helps Jim, he will be committing a serious crime. "People would call me a low down Ablitionist and despise me for keeping mum," says Huck, "but that don't make no difference. I ain't agoing to tell, and I ain't agoing back there anyways." An episode from Samuel Clemens's boyhood gives us a background for this part of the story. Tom Blankenship, the original Huck, had an older brother named Ben. In 1846, Ben found a runaway slave who had camped in a marshy area on the Illinois side of the river. Ben took food to the slave all summer and helped him survive. Besides the risk he ran for disobeying the law, Ben was also giving up the opportunity to earn a fifty-dollar reward for turning in the slave. It must have been a difficult choice for him, too.

When Huck meets Judith Loftus, he finds out that Jim's situation is even worse because men are coming to Jackson's Island to look for Jim. If Huck leaves without Jim, Jim is likely to be recaptured. For running away, Jim would surely be severely punished first, then sold. To further complicate the situation, Jim is suspected of Huck's murder, a crime he would likely hang for, because the people of St. Petersburg would never believe Jim's story that Huck was alive. In this first battle with his conscience, Huck knows that nothing that would happen to him for helping Jim would be as bad as what would happen to Jim if he did not help him.

"[Huck] listens to what goes on inside him. He is free to probe within his own heart, where is to be found whatever bit of divinity man has—what we know as his soul."
—Gladys Carmen Bellamy, 1950

Huck has a tougher struggle with his conscience when they are floating on the raft and getting nearer to Cairo. Jim talks about being free, and Huck begins to regret his decision to help him. Just when he has convinced himself that he must tell someone about the runaway slave, Huck has an encounter with some men on a raft who are looking for runaway slaves. Huck considers telling them about Jim. "I tried, for a second or two, to brace up and out with it," he says, "but I warn't man enough—hadn't the spunk of a rabbit." Instead of leading them to the raft, Huck makes the men believe his father is on the raft and is sick with smallpox.

Huck's greatest crisis comes when he realizes that the Dauphin has put Jim back into slavery by taking forty dollars for him from Silas Phelps. He realizes the seriousness of Jim's situation: although the runaway slave poster is bogus, he knows that whoever has Jim will treat him like a runaway. When his rightful owner is not located, Phelps could either keep Jim as his own slave, or sell him to someone else. Either way, Jim is unlikely to ever get back home to see his family again. Huck again battles his conscience. His upbringing and religious education tell him that the only moral choice is to turn Jim in. Huck decides to write to Miss Watson to tell her where Jim is, but struggles with that, too. Not only will Jim have to face the consequences of his attempt to escape, but Huck will also be shamed for his role in helping Jim. When he finally does write the letter, he says, "I felt good and all washed clean of sin for the first time I had ever felt so in my life, and I knowed I could pray now." Still, he does not feel right about this decision either, when he thinks about Jim not as a slave, but as the best friend he ever had. Finally, he decides that he must steal Jim out of slavery, even if it means he will go to hell.

Huck's crisis is important because it is his victory over his own conscience. Huck recognizes the difficulties of this troublesome inner voice, and says, "it don't make no difference whether you do right or wrong, a person's conscience ain't got no sense, and just goes for him *anyway*. If I had a yaller dog that didn't know no more than a person's conscience does I would pison him. It takes up more room than all the rest of a person's insides, and yet ain't no good, nohow." According to critic Stuart Hutchinson, "[Huck] does right, but cannot think right, and is thus the reverse of what is normally human. Our moral sense may allow us to think right, but it cannot guarantee we do right." Ultimately, Huck's real triumph is in the victory of his own inner morality that recognizes the humanity and goodness of Jim, and the true sin of treating people like property. Huck has chosen the higher good over the mistaken values of his society.

In this struggle, the reader can see that Twain, despite his protest in the opening "Notice," did have a moral to convey. Twain's own contempt for organized religion that is more "show" than truth comes through as Huck is caught in the conflict between his own heart and his logic, guided by his "education" in St. Petersburg. In his notebook in 1895, Twain described Huck's dilemma as the struggle between "a sound heart and a deformed conscience." Through Huck's narration, the author suggests that the morality man has manufactured to reinforce his own false values and laws is low and common when compared to the inner sense of good—and of God—that exists in the hearts of those who are not slaves to the influence of society's moral sense.

Slavery and *Huckleberry Finn*

Critic Neil Schmitz views *The Adventures of Huckleberry Finn* as reflecting three specific eras of American history: the 1850s, the Civil War, and the Reconstruction. The first part of the book, which was mostly written in 1876, reflects the pre-Civil war era of Clemens's childhood. The next section, Chapters Sixteen through Twenty-two, includes the feud and the killing of Boggs, and ends with the King and Duke being tarred and feathered. Schmitz compares this part to the violence of the Civil War and the defeat of the South. The last part, says Schmitz, "concerns setting free an already freed Jim, [and] symbolically enacts the Reconstruction as a nightmarish agony."

Unlike earlier books about the evils of slavery, such as Harriet Beecher Stowe's 1852 novel *Uncle Tom's Cabin*, Twain's purpose was not to change public opinion of the "peculiar institution" of slavery, as it was known. There was no real need to do that in the 1870s and 1880s, since slavery had ended many years earlier. The worst facts of slavery—cruel beatings, rape, murder, and inhumane working and living conditions—are never shown in Twain's novel. Compared to these cruelties, the slaves portrayed in *Huckleberry Finn* are treated mildly by their owners.

Twain uses the book to show the hypocrisy and immorality of the society that condoned the institution of slavery. In *Life on the Mississippi*, Twain blamed Scottish author Sir Walter Scott for bringing to the American South the romanticism and false aristocracy that "made every gentleman in the South a major or a colonel, or a general or a judge, before the war," and "created rank and caste down there, and also reverence for rank and caste, and pride and pleasure in them." Twain even goes so far as to say, "Sir Walter had so large a hand in making Southern character, as it existed before the war, that he is in great measure responsible for the war." It is not surprising then that the characters of Colonel Grangerford and Colonel Sherburn are important to the middle section of the book. It is also worth noting that in Chapters Twelve and Thirteen, a section inserted during 1883, the wrecked steamboat Huck and Jim explore is named *Walter Scott*. The thieves on board conspire against each other, but ultimately they all go down with the sinking ship.

Twain focuses on the responsibility of individuals and institutions such as the church that used their teachings to justify the dehumanizing and stereotyping of slaves. Although slavery was outlawed, these attitudes still persisted, even in the 1880s. In many areas of the South, free blacks were still treated as less than human and were denied their legal rights. They were subjected to fierce prejudice and often falsely accused of crimes. They were sometimes the victims of lynch mobs comprised of masked men.

Twain exposes these stereotypes through the eyes of Huck. When slave owners sold families apart, they tried to pretend that slaves did not love their children as much as white people did. As Huck and Jim float along on their raft, Huck tells us that Jim often moaned and cried for his wife and children at night. Huck is surprised that Jim cares about his family so much. "I do believe he cared just about as much for his people as white folks does for their'n," he says, and adds, "It don't seem natural, but I reckon it's so." The more noble characters of the book, such as the Wilks girls, do feel sympathy for their slaves who are separated from their families. Even Miss Watson, who was planning to sell Jim, eventually feels sorry for this decision.

Slaves were often characterized as being violent. Although Huck does not believe this, he uses this idea when he is looking for the Phelps farm to find Jim. In order to get more information about Jim's capture, he tells a boy, "I run across him in the woods about an hour or two ago, and he said if I hollered he'd cut my livers out." This detail makes his story more believable to this stranger, and he tells Huck the details of the wanted poster and describes the exchange of money when the Dauphin delivered Jim to the Phelpses.

Perhaps the worst offense against the slaves in the novel is the attitude that they are not even people. In Chapter Thirty-two, when Huck tells Aunt Sally that he had been delayed because the steamboat blew a cylinder-head, she is shocked.

"Good gracious! Anybody hurt?"

"No'm. Killed a nigger."

"Well, it's lucky, because sometimes people do get hurt."

Clearly, neither Sally nor Huck considers the victim "anybody."

Later, after Tom is wounded in the escape from the Phelpses, Jim gives up his freedom and reveals himself to the doctor in order to help him care for Tom. Although the Phelpses and their neighbors have been angry at Jim and some of them want to hang him, the doctor tells the story, and adds, "He ain't no bad nigger, gentlemen; that's what I think about him." As the others discuss the matter, they agree that Jim should have some reward, "So every one of them promised, right out and hearty, that they wouldn't cuss him no more." Significantly, Huck's assessment of Jim is not that he is a "good nigger," as the others say, but that, "I thought he had a good heart in him and was a good *man*" (*italics* added). Huck appears to be the only character who sees Jim for what he really is.

Religion in *Huckleberry Finn*

Samuel Clemens struggled for most of his life with his ideas about God and man's religious institutions. For Livy's sake, he tried to be a better person, but what he saw in church were people whose actions showed little of the morality they professed in their religious beliefs. Even as early as in *Innocents Abroad*, Twain criticized people whose narrow-minded religious beliefs caused them to adopt an attitude of moral superiority over others. In *Roughing It*, he commented on the corruption of the innocence and native culture of the Hawaiian people who had been "reformed" by missionaries who insisted that the natives give up their previous lifestyles and customs.

Perhaps Twain's most biting satire in *Huckleberry Finn* concerns religion. This satire begins in the first chapter.

Huck, with his practical thinking, has a difficult time accepting the religious doctrines of Miss Watson and the widow. Miss Watson sees heaven as she would like it—a place to sit around all day and play the harp and sing—not the type of place a young boy would find appealing. She insists that Huck will go to "the bad place" because he won't pay attention to his lessons and is superstitious. The widow, however, could "talk about Providence in a way to make a body's mouth water; but maybe the next day Miss Watson would take hold and knock it all down again."

Twain and Religion

"Pretended or misguided piety and other perversions of Christianity obviously head the list of counts in Mark Twain's indictment of the prewar South. And properly: for it is of course religion that stands at the center of the system of values in the society of this fictive world and by implication in all societies."

-Henry Nash Smith, 1962

Huck has a difficult time being interested in Bible stories once he figures out that the people in them lived long ago, "because I don't take no stock in dead people." By Chapter Three, the lesson turns to prayer. Again, because Huck is so practical, he has a hard time understanding the purpose of praying for spiritual gifts. He is disappointed that his answer to prayer is a fishing line but no hooks. After he has faked his murder, he is able to catch one of the loaves of bread that the townspeople sent out on the water to find his dead body. It is just what he wanted, since he is very hungry. He is able to reason that the widow or the parson had probably prayed for the bread to find him, and it had. It causes Huck to conclude that prayer does work, but only for just the "right kind" of people, certainly not for someone like him.

Every time people gather for a religious service in the

story, Twain uses the opportunity to show the shallowness of it. Few readers can miss the irony of the Grangerfords. They carry their guns to church and sit through a sermon on brotherly love. Afterward, "everybody said it was a good sermon, and they all talked it over going home, and had such a powerful lot to say about faith, and good works, and free grace, and preforeordestination. . . ." The next morning, the men all ride out to murder their neighbors. In Pokeville, the traveling preacher has his congregation so emotionally worked up with their responses of "amen!" and "glory hallelujah!" that they are eager to embrace the "pirate" and give him money to carry out his mission work to save the pirates of the Indian Ocean. At the Wilks funeral, the Baptist minister gives a sermon that Huck describes as "pison long and tiresome," but also includes the welcome diversion of a dog after a rat in the cellar.

In spite of the humor and irony he uses, Twain does not really ridicule the idea of belief in God or a higher morality. Nor does he ever attack a specific type of religion, even though he does make some references to the Baptists and Methodists. Instead he makes fun of the attitudes of these people who are confident of their own "goodness," but do not practice what they preach or see their fellow human beings with different skin colors as children of the same God.

Twain began Huck's story as a "boy's book" like *The Adventures of Tom Sawyer*, and *The Adventures of Huckleberry Finn* offers many elements that young readers would find appealing. Huck is a likable young hero. He dislikes stuffy clothing, school lessons, and Sunday school. He is loyal to his friends and tries to be good, but is able to tell lies when he needs to. He is able to do what many boys dream of: run away and be completely free. Huck and Jim, however, face a stronger opponent than the sinister Injun Joe of *Tom Sawyer*. They are in conflict with a slaveholding society motivated by greed. The serious issues included in *Huckleberry Finn* go beyond the level of understanding of

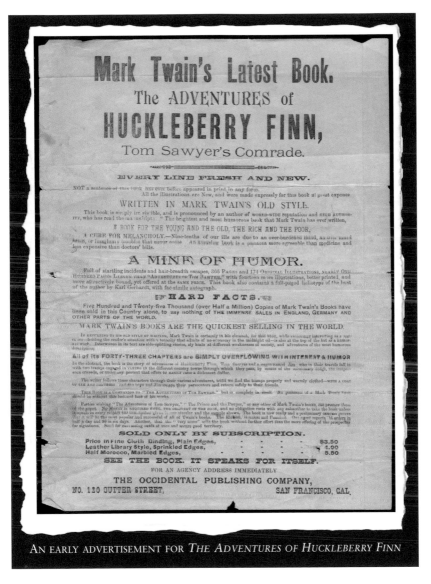

AN EARLY ADVERTISEMENT FOR *THE ADVENTURES OF HUCKLEBERRY FINN*

most young readers of *Tom Sawyer*. Twain's treatment of the "adult" issues of racism, hypocrisy in religion, and corrupt society has been discussed by students, teachers, and critics far more than Twain could have predicted in 1873, and they are still the focus of controversy today.

Chapter 2

The Critical Heritage of *Huckleberry Finn*

"All modern literature comes from one book by Mark Twain called *Huckleberry Finn*. It's the best book we've had. All American writing comes from that. There was nothing before. There has been nothing as good since."
—Ernest Hemingway, *Green Hills of Africa*, 1935

THE ADVENTURES OF HUCKLEBERRY FINN was controversial from the very beginning. Because the book begins by continuing the story of *Tom Sawyer*, many people believed it to be intended for young readers. With this belief, some of the language, scenes of nudity, and violence were judged to be inappropriate. The library in Concord, Massachusetts, decided not to include the book in its collection. According to a news item in a Boston newspaper, one of the library committee members said the book "contains but little humor, and that of a very coarse type." The committee judged the book as being "more suited to the slums than to intelligent, respectable people."

In his typical way, Twain responded to this news in a letter to the secretary of the Concord Free Trade Club, calling the library committee's decision a "generous action," which would surely increase sales, because "one book in a public library prevents the sale of a sure ten and a possible hundred of its mates."

Critics have argued the merits of the book since 1885, and are still divided in their opinions today. They disagree about the likability and believability of the characters, plot, and language of the book.

As the main character, Huck is honest and good-hearted. His plain speech and overall gentleness are likable. Huck's inner struggle progresses through the book, and each time he makes a decision to defend Jim, it is a more difficult, and therefore stronger, decision than the one before. Still, some readers are disappointed that Huck does not really demonstrate growth and change in his character by the end of the novel. Literary critic Richard Chase, in his 1957 book entitled *The American Novel and Its Tradition*, remarks, "There is no real change in Huck Finn during the course of the book, except that he comes to adopt, as he reflects on his duty to Jim, a morality based on New Testament ethic rather than the convention of his time and place." Although Chase does not explain what he means by his term "New Testament ethic," the reader might wonder if that ethic includes the idea of treating others as one would like to be treated, as Jesus told his disciples in the New Testament book of Luke. If so, then Huck has not even changed enough to fully practice this.

While Huck believes that Jim should be free, he is not truly ready to treat Jim as he would wish to be treated himself. If so, he would not allow Tom to inflict such misery upon his friend during their rescue plan. In fact, he expresses more sympathy for the treatment of the Duke and Dauphin than he does for Jim, whose only "crime" is his desire for freedom. Also, Huck never really rejects the beliefs of his society enough to truly see the immorality of slavery. While he does accept the basic humanity of Jim, it is never clear that he feels the same about any of the other slaves in the book. According to critic Stuart Hutchinson, "Even Miss Watson's remorse can be seen as a critique both of Huck's incapacity for moral sense with respect to slavery, and also of the book's fundamental disbelief in development. Miss Watson gives Jim freedom; Huck gets him nowhere."

At the end of the book, Huck's intention is to run away again, this time to the West, in order to flee Aunt Sally's determination to civilize him. He does not want to go back to St. Petersburg, where he would have to face the judgment of the townspeople for his decision to help Jim. Nor does he want to return to the care of the widow and his other friends.

Of course, throughout the book, "civilization" has been a corrupting influence on individual morality, so it is not surprising that Huck wants no more to do with it. Richard P. Adams published an analysis of the book in which he suggested that Huck's "death" in Chapter Seven is symbolic of his separation from his society and his rebirth with the ability to see that society with its flaws. Considered this way, Huck's decision to run away makes sense, because he could never return to the previous lack of awareness that allowed him to accept and be a part of that society. Hutchinson says that the ending's lack of resolution is a reflection of Huck's character. "Huck must remain fugitive because the book's adventures never entail, let alone reach, a clarifying destination. [Huck] remains inconsistent as a character, telling some jokes but not getting others, being an innocent boy but a shrewd and cynical liar, committed and oblivious to Jim."

Jim is an even more controversial character than Huck. Jim is lovable and human, but still subservient, ignorant, and too eager to agree with the foolish schemes of Tom.

Many African-American readers dislike the portrayal of Jim for these reasons. African-American novelist Ralph Ellison commented, "I could imagine myself as Huck Finn, but not, though I racially identified with him as . . . Jim, who struck me as a white man's inadequate portrait of a slave." Robert O'Meally, literature professor at Columbia University, first read the book as a young man, and has taught it in his classes for many years. He agrees with Ellison, saying, "[I]t was definitely Huck whose point of view I adopted, while Jim remained a shadowy construction whose buffoonery and will to cooperate with white folks' foolishness embarrassed and infuriated me." Some critics in Twain's time and even today claim that his writings were racist. Not all agree, however. Booker T. Washington, born a slave in 1856, but later a well-known educator and an acquaintance of Clemens, said, "I do not believe any one can read this story closely, without becoming aware of the deep sympathy of the author in Jim."

Critic Peter Messent comments on the change in Jim's role in the novel. Early in the journey, Jim is a significant presence on the raft and he reveals his humanity through his talk about his children. He often assumes the role of parent, taking care of Huck, taking his watch at night, and calling for him in the fog. Huck acknowledges Jim's humanity when he apologizes to Jim after playing a trick on him.

Once they pass Cairo, however, Jim's power and presence diminishes. He disappears during the Grangerford episode, then gives up his adult role, becoming subject first to Huck, then the king and duke, and even to Tom Sawyer. Although Jim takes the first step toward his freedom when he runs away from Miss Watson at the end of the book, Jim makes no efforts in his own quest for freedom, other than cooperating with the two boys and allowing them to take care of it for him. While readers would not wish harm to this character, Twain created in Jim such a strong inner desire for his freedom that it might be more satisfying for him to take a more active role in obtaining it. Still, Twain is careful to place the blame for Jim's situation on white society. If Jim were to act out in rebellion against his oppressors, some readers, especially those of Twain's time, would interpret those actions as illustrating the very stereotypes Twain sought to disprove.

The relationship between Jim and Huck is also more complicated than it may seem at first. Through the years, some critics have considered the raft, adrift on the river apart from society, as a place of innocence like the Garden of Eden. Huck and Jim find their food in the river and along its banks, and they have no need of clothing as they travel at night, so they are naked most of the time. They look at the stars and discuss the mystery of creation. They talk about all kinds of things and enjoy the sights, sounds and smells of their environment (Chapter Nineteen).

Later critics, however, have pointed out that the raft is not free of the influence of society, nor is it free of conflict. Neil Schmitz points out that even on the raft, Huck and Jim are not completely honest and trusting with each other. Jim knows that Pap is dead, but does not tell Huck, perhaps because he fears Huck would then have no reason to run away, and would not continue the journey with him. Likewise, Huck realizes that the king and duke are imposters but chooses not to tell Jim, perhaps because "of his fear that Jim will react to the truth by running away." Peter Messent also recognizes the conflict, but says, "In many ways the raft functions as an estranged or alienated social world where Huck and Jim depart from the accepted norms of interracial behavior. . . . On the raft, not all, but some of the time, the interaction of black and white without fear, prejudice or constraint can be accommodated."

The plot of *The Adventures of Huckleberry Finn* is one of the most debated aspects of the book. The story contains many good episodes, but most are miniature stories that stand alone. In a way they are like pearls strung together be part of one strand, but not really connected to each other. Critic Bernard DeVoto commented that "No more than Huck and the river's motion gives continuity to a series of episodes which are in essence only developed anecdotes." In fact, many of the events in the middle of the book could be changed in their order without really changing the story itself. Critic Lionel Trilling, however, believed that the unity of the book comes from the river itself. In his view, the river is a major character in the book, and is, in fact, a kind of god, providing a spiritual center that Huck cannot find within his society. Leo Marx, however disagrees with Trilling's assessment, saying that the river "provides motion; it is a means by which Huck and Jim . . . continue their journey. The river cannot, does not, supply purpose."

But readers may struggle with a question that is central to the book: What is the purpose of their journey? The obvious answer is freedom, but that may not be as simple as it seems. Peter Messent asserts that one major conflict of the novel concerns the reality that Huck and Jim have different ideas of what freedom is. For Jim, freedom is escape from slavery, the ability to leave the raft and return to society and to his family as a free man. For Huck, freedom is life on the raft, escape from society, and the formation of a new "family" with Jim. They make a plan to sell the raft once they get to Cairo and travel on a steamboat up the Ohio River. In this plan, Huck's role ends once Jim has achieved his goal. According to Messent, "Huck would much prefer to stay on the raft while Jim wants to get off it. For Huck, the very meaning of the raft—freedom, ease, safety, 'home' is conditional on Jim's presence."

In fact, the purpose of their journey, freedom for Jim and for Huck, is completely lost from the time they pass Cairo in the fog until the point where Tom re enters the story. This final section of the book is perhaps the most controversial.

Some readers like the ending of the book, because it is almost like returning to St. Petersburg because of the presence of Tom Sawyer. Others dislike it because it takes Jim's serious quest for freedom and turns it into a comedy sketch. The final scene contains some of the book's best humor, but also is degrading to Jim, and tests the reader's acceptance of the truth of the serious nature of the story. Despite these objections, some readers praise the ending. Author T. S. Eliot defends Twain's ending as necessary to the unity of the book. He insists, "[I]t is right that the mood of the end of the book should bring us back to the beginning."

The final episode lacks the depth of emotion of other parts of the book. Henry Nash Smith says, "The perplexing final sequence on the Phelps plantation is best regarded as a maneuver by which Mark Twain beats his way back from incipient tragedy to the comic resolution called for by the original conception of the story." Many readers feel that it takes away the heroic quality of Jim's escape, since we discover at the end that he is already free. He has not achieved his freedom through any action of his own, or even with Huck's help, but through the actions of Miss Watson, who was only influenced by her own sense of guilt, not by a sense of Jim's humanity. Marx asserts an even more serious criticism of the ending: "In the closing episode, however, we lose sight of Jim in the maze of farcical invention. He ceases to be a man. . . . These antics divest Jim, as well as Huck, of much of his dignity and individuality."

Of course, without Tom, Huck himself could have freed Jim the first night he arrived at the Phelps farm. Although the white boy and black slave would still face dangers in the South, their strong friendship and Huck's cleverness had certainly helped them out in the first part of the book and could lead to a different ending. Some critics have suggested that Tom's elaborate, confusing, and slow plan to free Jim was perhaps intentionally designed to suggest the struggle for freedom slaves faced for many years after the Civil War. As O'Meally says, "The book slows down, then, to suggest the miserable slowness of the process of gaining black freedom in America—stuck in a mire of what might be termed Tom Sawyerism. We can't stop reading until the novel's end, but these last chapters are an agony!"

Also, the ending provides no real resolution for Huck. He is ready to run away again and forget his attachment to Jim, the widow, or anyone else. He is also never allowed to really demonstrate the inner changes of his character, if indeed these changes have taken place. Still, Eliot believed that the vague ending of the book was the only one possible for Huck. "For Huckleberry Finn, neither a tragic nor a happy ending would be suitable. No worldly success or social satisfaction, no domestic consummation would be worthy of him; a tragic end also would reduce him to the level of those whom we pity. Huck Finn must come from nowhere and be bound for nowhere."

Even at the end, when Jim has acquired his "freedom" from Miss Watson, we might well ask what that freedom will really be like, if Jim returns to St. Petersburg or any other slave-holding community in pre-Civil War America. Although technically "free," he will certainly not be "equal"—not as long as people with ideas like Pap's are around. Even in the post-Civil War South of the 1880s, Twain saw that "freedom" and "equality" were two very different concepts. In this light, Jim's "happy ending" does not look quite the same. While Jim and Huck had briefly enjoyed both freedom and equality, such ideas were not easy to realize in society for either free slave or orphaned white boy. Considered that way, perhaps Huck's decision to "light out for the territory" is simply a continuation of his own quest for freedom.

Language

Twain's use of language in *Huckleberry Finn* and other books was different from that of most writers of his time. Most writers who expected to be considered "literary" wrote in a style that was more formal, and cultured, and sounded much like writers in Europe. From his earliest days in journalism, Twain's writing had always been straightforward and casual. Later, as a lecturer, Twain charmed audiences with his homespun humor and slightly Southern drawl. Because Huck is the narrator of the story, Twain had to use a voice that reflected the simple, barely educated, and honest character of the son of the town drunk. He spoke ungrammatically, using words like "ain't" and phrases like "I knowed what was the matter."

"He has drawn the national type, interpreted the national character. For that service we may be grateful. And he has taught unobtrusively, but not the less powerfully, the virtues of common sense and honest manliness. If it comes to a choice, these are better than refinement."

—Charles Miner Thompson, 1897

At the beginning of the book, Twain includes a note about the different dialects, naming and describing them, and explaining his "personal familiarity with these several forms of speech." He felt this note was necessary because "without it many readers would suppose that all these characters were trying to talk alike and not succeeding." With the rapidly expanding boundaries of the United States, Americans were beginning to recognize and embrace the differences in language in other parts of the country outside of the original colonies. Many critics have praised Twain's keen ear for the subtleties of dialect. Bernard DeVoto praised Twain's use of dialect, and claimed, "no equal sensitiveness to American speech has ever been brought to fiction." Others of Mark Twain's time also used dialect, but, according to Lionel Trilling, "no one could play with it nearly so well . . . the subtle variations of speech of *Huckleberry Finn*, of which Mark Twain was justly proud, are still part of the liveliness and flavor of the book."

"His humor is the national humor—so wild and free and lawless in its adventures, that it seems to the uncultured mind too good to be literature."

—Theodore De Laguna, 1898

To Ban or Not to Ban?

Despite this type of praise, few books of the nineteenth century have generated as much controversy as *Huckleberry Finn*. It began with the Concord Library, but it did not end there. Critics of Twain's time were divided in their response to the book. Some praised it; some deplored it. A reviewer in the *Boston Evening Traveller*, echoing Shakespeare, concluded that "*Huckleberry Finn* appears to be singularly flat, stale, and unprofitable." Likewise, the *San Francisco Daily Examiner* said, "there is little to be said in the book's favor. . . . It is very much of the same character as many of the author's Pacific Coast sketches, in the utter absence of truth." A review in *Life* magazine used its own satire to discuss Twain's humor. It talked about Huck's killing of a pig and smearing its blood to fake his own death as a "little joke" that "can be repeated by any smart boy for the amusement of his fond parents." The biggest objection of librarians and teachers was the main character's poor use of language and his bad behavior, which included lying, stealing, and running away from home.

Other critics sang its praises. The reviewer for *The Atlanta Constitution* said, "It is difficult to believe that the critics who have condemned the book as coarse, vulgar, and inartistic can have read it." The *Hartford Daily Times* declared, "It is a good book. . . . It teaches, without seeming to do it, the virtue of honest simplicity, directness, and truth." A review in The *Hartford Courant* announced, "Mr. Clemens has made a very distinct literary advance over *Tom Sawyer*, as an interpreter of human nature and a contributor to our stock of original pictures of American life." The *Saturday Review* praised Twain's characterization in this way: "That Mr. Clemens draws from life, and yet lifts his work from the domain of the photograph to the region of art, is evident to any one who will give his work the honest attention it deserves."

In 1905, the librarians of the Brooklyn, New York, public library removed both *Tom Sawyer* and *Huckleberry Finn* from the children's department, although they kept the books in the adult collection of the library. They determined that the behaviors of the boys in those books presented poor examples for children. Twain responded in a letter comparing the moral characters of the boys in his books to the characters of Solomon and David in the Bible.

Readers and scholars today are as divided in their opinions as those of Twain's day. *Huckleberry Finn* has been banned by some schools and libraries, but is included in the curriculum of many others. For the last fifty years, the main complaint against the book has been its stereotypical portrayal of the slaves in the book and the frequent use of the word "nigger." Both teachers and students have difficulty dealing with this aspect of the book.

Historically, the word "nigger" was clearly a part of everyday speech for people in many parts of the country. Like many words in our language, it had different shades of meaning, depending upon the speaker, the situation, and the tone and intent of it. Some characters in the book use it as a demeaning term; others, like Huck, use it because it is the only word they know to describe a person with dark skin. In the 1840s, the time of the setting of the novel, this is true to life. For Twain to have only the "bad" people in the book use the term would have been unrealistic. The word strikes a sour note, however, with the sensibilities of readers of the twentieth and twenty-first centuries. For many readers, use of the word "nigger" is only one aspect of the problem of racial attitudes in *Huckleberry Finn*.

Tom and Huck Banned

Mark Twain wrote this letter to a librarian of the Brooklyn, New York, public library, where *Tom Sawyer* and *Huckleberry Finn* had recently been removed from the children's section of the library because the behavior of the characters was considered unsuitable for children to read:

21 5th Avenue
Nov. 21, '05.

Dear Sir,—I am greatly troubled by what you say. I wrote *Tom Sawyer* & *Huck Finn* for adults exclusively, & it always distresses me when I find that boys & girls have been allowed access to them. The mind that becomes soiled in youth can never again be washed clean. I know this by my own experience, & to this day I cherish an unappeasable bitterness against the unfaithful guardians of my young life, who not only permitted but compelled me to read an unexpurgated Bible through before I was 15 years old. None can do that and ever draw a clean, sweet breath again this side of the grave. Ask that young lady—she will tell you so.

Most honestly do I wish that I could say a softening word or two in defense of Huck's character since you wish it, but really, in my opinion, it is no better than those of Solomon, David, & the rest of the sacred brotherhood.

If there is an unexpurgated in the Children's Department, won't you please help that young woman remove *Tom* & *Huck* from that questionable companionship?

Sincerely yours,
S. L. Clemens

Huckleberry Finn and Slavery

Terrell Dempsey, an attorney in Hannibal, Missouri, has made a study of Hannibal and the culture of slavery in which young Samuel Clemens was raised. In his book, *Searching for Jim: Slavery in Sam Clemens's World*, he concludes,

> I know *Huckleberry Finn* is flawed. It must be. Clemens was white. He never suffered as a slave. He did not personally know the day-to-day, cradle to grave degradation experienced by the men, women, and children who made up one-quarter of the population and labored for the other three-quarters. But Clemens is one of the best we have. His gift is that he cared deeply and watched closely. He had a genius for nuance and language. At a time when most white people thought African-Americans weren't quite as human as they, he knew better.

In the 1950s and 1960s, as the Civil Rights movement began to gain momentum, many schools began reconsidering the use of *Huckleberry Finn* in classrooms. In 1957, the public schools in New York City decided to drop the book from its list of approved texts, although the book remained available in libraries in the district. In 1962, a stage adaptation of the story in a high school in San Francisco brought protests from parents and a boycott by the National Association for the Advancement of Colored People because African-American students were cast in the roles of slaves. In 1966, African-American students at the University of Massachusetts protested the book as required reading.

In the mid-1990s, the book was repeatedly challenged in complaints to school districts across the nation. The issue spurred a court battle in Tempe, Arizona, when a parent charged that reading the book resulted in racial slurs and graffiti directed at her daughter and other African-American students at the girl's high school. That court case continued up to a federal appeals court, where it finally ruled in favor of the school district, claiming that it is not the place of the court to determine curriculum, and that banning books may constitute a violation of students' rights.

"If we'd eradicated the problem of racism in our society, *Huckleberry Finn* would be the easiest book in the world to teach."
—writer David Bradley, 2000

Despite the court's ruling, the case brought national attention to the use of *The Adventures of Huckleberry Finn* in the classroom. It also opened the issue to extended discussion and debate among educators about the value of the book. An online bulletin board sponsored by the National Council of Teachers of English attracted comments from teachers about their decision to either include or omit the book from their classes. Some felt that with the proper historical background and sensitivity, the book could be a good teaching tool. Others felt that the controversy, combined with the book's flaws of plot and character development, did not make it worth defending to parents and students.

"I believe that [*Huckleberry Finn*] will be read by human beings of all ages, not as a solemn duty but for the honest love of it, and over and over again, long after every book written in America between the years 1800 and 1860 . . . has disappeared entirely save as a classroom fossil."
—H. L. Mencken, 1913

In 2000, public television station WGBH Boston sponsored a program on PBS called *Born to Trouble: Adventures of Huck Finn*, in which the merits of the novel in the classroom were discussed by professors and scholars. WGBH produced educational materials for teachers in conjunction with the film, in order to help them use the book in their classroom as a springboard for frank discussion of racial issues. Jocelyn Chadwick, assistant professor at Harvard's Graduate School of Education, says, "Through the controversy surrounding this book alone, Twain brings into schools what all of us in the country desperately need, yet fear most: discussion—frank discussions—about race, race relations, interracial relations, race language, racial stereotypes and profiling, and ultimately, true and unadulterated racial equality."

Chronology

1835
Samuel Langhorn Clemens born November 30 in Florida, Missouri, to John Marshall Clemens and Jane Lampton Clemens

1839
John Clemens moves the family to Hannibal, Missouri

1847
John Clemens dies; Samuel leaves school to work as printer's apprentice

1850–1853
Works for older brother, Orion Clemens, at *Hannibal Journal*

1853
Leaves Hannibal to work as typesetter in St. Louis, Philadelphia, and New York, before returning briefly in 1854, then traveling throughout the Midwest for several years

1857
Signs on as cub pilot with riverboat captain Horace Bixby

1859
Earns steamboat pilot's license

1861
Returns briefly to Missouri to join confederate militia group, then travels to Nevada territory with brother Orion; works as clerk for Nevada Territorial Legislature

1862–1863
Begins writing humorous articles for *Virginia City Territorial Enterprise*; adopts pen name Mark Twain

1864
Moves to San Francisco, begins writing for the literary magazine, *The Golden Era*, and San Francisco newspaper, *Morning Call*, until fired in October

1865
Lives in mining camp in Calaveras County, California; writes short story "Jim Smiley and his Jumping Frog," which is published and reprinted as "The Celebrated Jumping Frog of Calaveras County"

1866
Travels to Sandwich Islands (later named Hawaii), as correspondent for *Sacramento Union*; begins first lecture tour

1867
Moves to New York; sails on *Quaker City* and sends travel correspondence to *Alta California*; meets Olivia Langdon; begins job as secretary for Nevada Senator William Stewart in Washington, D.C.; *The Celebrated Jumping Frog of Calaveras County and Other Sketches* published

1868
Continues lecturing throughout the West; becomes engaged to Olivia Langdon

1869
Publishes *Innocents Abroad*; continues lecturing; becomes part owner of *Buffalo Express* newspaper

1870
Samuel and Olivia are married; they move to Buffalo, New York, where Samuel works for *Buffalo Express*; son, Langdon Clemens, is born

1871
Samuel sells home and newspaper and moves the family to Elmira, New York; later moves to Hartford, Connecticut

1872
Daughter Susy born; Langdon dies; *Roughing It* published

1873
Plans new home in Hartford; travels to England

1874
Clemens family moves in temporarily with Livy's sister at Quarry Farm; daughter Clara is born

1876
Adventures of Tom Sawyer is released; works on *The Adventures of Huckleberry Finn* and pieces for *Life on the Mississippi*

1878–1879
Clemens family travels in Europe

1880
A Tramp Abroad is published; daughter Jean is born

1881–1885
Publishes *The Prince and the Pauper, Life on the Mississippi,*

Huckleberry Finn; goes into business with nephew Charley Webster to form publishing company; Webster and Company publishes *Personal Memoirs of U. S. Grant*

1886–1894
Invests in Paige Compositor and continues to pour money into it until he is forced to declare bankruptcy; travels between United States and Europe, both for Livy's health and to relieve the financial burden of the Hartford home; Webster and Company declares bankruptcy

1895–1900
Travels on world lecture tour to repay debts; daughter Susy dies (1896); Clemens family lives in several cities in Europe

1901
Moves the family to Riverdale, New York; receives honorary Doctorate of Letters degree from Yale

1902
Livy becomes ill with heart problems; Samuel receives honorary degree from the University of Missouri

1904
Livy dies; Clara suffers nervous breakdown

1906
Clemens appoints Albert Bigelow Paine to be his official biographer; Paine moves into the Clemens home; Clemens addresses Congress to speak for stronger copyright laws

1907
Clemens travels to England to receive honorary degree from Oxford

1908
Samuel and Jean move to Stormfield in Redding, Connecticut

1909
Clemens begins to suffer from chest pains; Clara marries; Jean suffers an epileptic seizure on Christmas Eve

1910
Makes final trip to Bermuda; dies on April 21 at Stormfield

Works

Mark Twain's writings include many newspaper articles, short stories, speeches, essays, and plays, as well as novels. Listed below are his most recognized works.

1850s
Writes travel letters and other pieces for the *Hannibal Journal*, *Keokuk Post*, and other newspapers

1862–1865
Writes for newspapers: *Virginia City Territorial Enterprise*, *San Francisco Daily Morning Call*, and *Alta California*

1867
Celebrated Jumping Frog of Calaveras County

1869
Innocents Abroad

1872
Roughing It

1873
The Gilded Age (written with Charles Dudley Warner)

1876
The Adventures of Tom Sawyer

1880
A Tramp Abroad

1881
The Prince and the Pauper

1883
Life on the Mississippi

1885
The Adventures of Huckleberry Finn

1889
A Connecticut Yankee in King Arthur's Court

1892
The American Claimant

1894
The Tragedy of Pudd'nhead Wilson and the Comedy of those Extraordinary Twins

1895
Personal Recollections of Joan of Arc

1897
Following the Equator

1899
"The Man that Corrupted Hadleyburg" and Other Stories and Essays

1902
"Double-Barrelled Detective Story"

1905
Extracts from Eve's Diary

1909
Captain Stormfield's Visit to Heaven (written in 1868, first published in *Harper's Magazine* in 1907–1908)

1962
Letters from the Earth (written in 1909)

Notes

Part I *The Life of Samuel Clemens*

Chapter 1
p. 9, Dawidziak, Mark, ed. *Mark My Words: Mark Twain on Writing*. New York: St. Martin's Press, 1996.

p. 10, Mencken, H. L. "The Burden of Humor," *Smart Set*, Feb. 1913. BoondocksNet.com, 1995–2005. www.boondocksnet.com/twaintexts/mencken1302.html (accessed January 18, 2005).

p. 10, Thompson, Charles Miner. "Mark Twain as an Interpreter of American Character," *Atlantic Monthly*, April 1897. BoondocksNet.com, 1995–2005. www.boondocksnet.com/twaintexts/mt_atlantic9704.html (accessed January 18, 2005).

p. 11, Neider, Charles, ed. *The Autobiography of Mark Twain*. New York: Harper & Brothers Publishers, 1959.

p. 13, Neider. *The Autobiography of Twain*.

p. 14, Neider. *The Autobiography of Twain*.

p. 14, Clemens, Samuel. *Life on the Mississippi*, Vol. 7 of *Complete Works of Mark Twain*. Authorized Edition. New York: Harper & Brothers, 1917.

p. 16, Clemens, Samuel. "Missouri University Speech," in *Mark Twain's Speeches*. New York: Harper & Brothers Publishers, 1910.

p. 17, Wector, Dixon. *Sam Clemens of Hannibal*. Boston: Houghton Mifflin Co., 1952.

p. 18, Neider. *The Autobiography of Twain*.

p. 18, Kaplan, Justin. *Mark Twain and His World*. New York: Simon and Schuster, 1974.

pp. 18–20, Armstrong, C. J. "Mark Twain's Early Writings Discovered," *Missouri Historical Review*, Vol. 24, no. 4 (July 1930).

pp. 20, 23, Neider. *The Autobiography of Twain*.

pp. 23–25, Neider. *The Autobiography of Twain*.

Chapter 2
p. 27, Paine, Albert Bigelow. *Mark Twain: A Biography, Three Volumes*, vol. 1. New York: Harper & Brothers Publishers, 1912.

p. 27, Neider, Charles, ed. *The Autobiography of Mark Twain*. New York: Harper & Brothers Publishers, 1959.

p. 27, Clemens, Samuel. "The Private History of a Campaign that Failed," in *A Pen Warmed-up in Hell*. Frederick Anderson, ed. New York: Harper and Row, 1972.

p. 28, Clemens, Samuel. *Roughing It*. Berkeley: University of California Press, 1972.

p. 31, Neider, Charles, ed. *The Autobiography of Mark Twain*. New York: Harper & Brothers Publishers, 1959.

p. 32, Neider. *The Autobiography of Twain*.

p. 34, Clemens, Samuel. "Mark Twain's First Appearance," in *Mark Twain's Speeches*. New York: Harper & Brothers Publishers, 1910.

p. 36, Clemens, Samuel. *Innocents Abroad, or The New Pilgrims' Progress*. Hartford, CT: American Publishing Company, 1871.

p. 37, Clemens. *Innocents Abroad*.

p. 38, Kaplan, Justin. *Mr. Clemens and Mark Twain*. New York: Simon and Schuster, 1966.

Chapter 3
p. 42, Neider, Charles, ed. *The Autobiography of Mark Twain*. New York: Harper & Brothers Publishers, 1959.

p. 43, Neider. *Autobiography of Twain*.

p. 45, Lutz, Norma Jean. "Biography of Mark Twain," in *Bloom's Biocritiques: Mark Twain*, Harold Bloom, ed. Philadelphia: Chelsea House, 2003.

p. 46, 48, Neider. *Autobiography of Twain*.

p. 48, Clemens, Samuel. "The Babies," in *Mark Twain's Speeches*, New York: Harper & Brothers Publishers, 1910.

p. 50, Clemens, Samuel. "The Story of a Speech," in *Speeches*.

p. 50, Howells, William Dean. *My Mark Twain: Reminiscences and Criticisms*. New York: Harper & Brothers Publishers, 1910.

pp. 52–53, Clemens, Susy. *Biography of Mark Twain*. BoondocksNet.com, 1995–2005. www.boondocksnet.com/twaintexts/susy/ (accessed January 18, 2005).

p. 53, Neider. *Autobiography of Twain*.

p. 55, Ward, Geoffrey, Dayton Duncan, and Ken Burns. *Mark Twain: An Illustrated Biography*. New York: Alfred A. Knopf, 2001.

p. 55, Lang, Andrew. "The Art of Mark Twain," in *Critical Essays on Mark Twain, 1867–1910*, Louis J. Budd, ed. Boston: G. K. Hall & Co., 1982.

pp. 55, 57, Ward, Duncan, and Burns.

p. 58, Dawidziak, Mark, ed. *Mark My Words: Mark Twain on Writing*. New York: St. Martin's Press, 1996.

p. 58, Dawidziak. *Mark My Words*.

p. 58, Neider. *Autobiography of Twain*.

p. 58, Clemens, Samuel. "Statistics," in *Speeches*.

p. 59, Ward, Duncan, and Burns.

Chapter 4

p. 60, Paine, Albert Bigelow. *Mark Twain: A Biography, Three Volumes*, Vol. 2. New York: Harper & Brothers Publishers, 1912.

p. 61, Paine. *Twain: A Biography*, Vol. 2.

p. 62, Dawidziak, Mark, ed. *Mark My Words: Mark Twain on Writing*. New York: St. Martin's Press, 1996.

p. 63, Clemens, Samuel. "A New German Word," in *Mark Twain's Speeches*. New York: Harper & Brothers Publishers, 1910.

p. 64, Howells, William Dean. *My Mark Twain: Reminiscences and Criticisms*. New York: Harper & Brothers Publishers, 1910.

p. 66, Kaplan, Justin. *Mr. Clemens and Mark Twain: A Biography*. New York: Simon and Schuster, 1966.

pp 66–67, Kaplan. *Clemens and Twain*.

pp. 66 67, Dawidziak. *Mark My Words*

p. 67, Clemens. "Seventieth Birthday," in *Speeches*.

p. 68, Howells. *My Mark Twain*.

p. 68, Clemens. "Dress Reform and Copyright," in *Speeches*.

p. 69, Lystra, Karen. *Dangerous Intimacy: The Untold Story of Mark Twain's Final Years*. Berkeley: University of California Press, 2004.

p. 69, Howells. *My Mark Twain*.

p. 70, Paine. *Twain: A Biography*, Vol 3.

pp. 70–72, Quick, Dorothy. *Enchantment: A Little Girl's Friendship with Mark Twain*. Norman: University of Oklahoma Press, 1961.

pp. 72, 74, Lystra. *Dangerous Intimacy*.

p. 75, Anonymous article in *Baltimore Sun*, April 22, 1910, in *Critical Essays on Mark Twain, 1867–1910*, Louis J. Budd, ed. Boston: G. K. Hall & Co., 1982, p. 227.

Part II *A Reader's Guide to* The Adventures of Huckleberry Finn

Chapter 1

p. 79, Anderson, Frederick, William Gibson, and Henry Nash Smith. *Selected Mark Twain–Howells Letters, 1872–1910.* Cambridge, MA: Belknap Press, 1967.

p. 79, Clemens, Samuel. "Notice," in *The Adventures of Huckleberry Finn* (Centennial Facsimile Edition). New York: Harper & Row, 1987.

p. 79, Lang, Andrew. "The Art of Mark Twain," in *Critical Essays on Mark Twain, 1867–1910*, Louis J. Budd, ed. Boston: G. K. Hall & Co., 1982.

p. 86, Clemens. *Huckleberry Finn.*

pp. 86–87, Anderson, Gibson, and Smith. *Twain–Howells Letters.*

pp. 88–89, Blair, Walter. *Mark Twain & Huck Finn.* Berkeley: University of California Press, 1960.

p. 90, Blair. *Twain & Finn.*

pp. 90–91, Messent, Peter. *Mark Twain.* New York: St. Martin's Press, 1997.

p. 91, Neider, Charles, ed. *The Autobiography of Mark Twain.* New York: Harper & Brothers Publishers, 1959.

p. 91, Schmitz, Neil. "Mark Twain's Civil War: Humor's Reconstructive Writing," in *Bloom's Biocritiques: Mark Twain*, Harold Bloom, ed. Philadelphia: Chelsea House, 2003.

p. 91, Schmitz. "Twain's Civil War."

p. 92, Howells, William Dean. *My Mark Twain: Reminiscences and Criticisms.* New York: Harper & Brothers, 1910.

p. 92, Anderson, Gibson, and Smith. *Twain-Howells Letters.*

p. 93, Neider. *Autobiography of Twain.*

pp. 94–98, Clemens. *Huckleberry Finn.*

p. 99, Zwick, Jim. "Should *Huckleberry Finn* be Banned?" BoondocksNet.com, 1995–2005. www.boondocksnet.com/twainwww/essays/huck_ banned9703.html (accessed January 18, 2005).

p. 100, Neider. *Autobiography of Twain.*

p. 101, Clemens. *Huckleberry Finn.*

p. 101, Bellamy, Gladys Carmen. "Roads to Freedom," in *Twentieth Century Interpretations of* Adventures of Huckleberry Finn, Claude M. Simpson, ed. Englewood Cliffs, NJ: Prentice Hall, 1968.

p. 102, Clemens. *Huckleberry Finn.*

p. 103, Hutchinson, Stuart. "Introduction to *The Adventures of Tom Sawyer* & *The Adventures of Huckleberry Finn,*" *Bloom's Biocritiques: Mark Twain,* Harold Bloom, ed., Philadelphia: Chelsea House, 2003.

p. 103, Clemens, Samuel. Notebook, 1895. *Mark Twain Scrapbook.* Corporation for Public Broadcasting, no date. www.pbs.org/marktwain/scrapbook/05_gilded_age/page4 .html (accessed January 11, 2005).

pp. 103–104, Schmitz. "Twain's Civil War."

p. 104, Clemens, Samuel. *Life on the Mississippi*, vol. 7 of *Complete Works of Mark Twain,* Authorized edition. New York: Harper & Brothers Publishers, 1917.

pp. 106–107, Clemens. *Huckleberry Finn.*

p. 107, Smith, Henry Nash. *Mark Twain: The Development of a Writer.* Cambridge, Mass: Belknap Press, 1962.

pp. 107–108, Clemens. *Huckleberry Finn.*

Chapter 2

p. 110, Zwick, Jim. "Huckleberry Finn Debated." BoondocksNet.com, 1995–2005. www.boondocksnet.com/twainwww/hf_debate.html (accessed January 18, 2005).

p. 110, Unsigned article reprinted in Boston *Transcript*, April 4, 1885, quoted in *Huckleberry Finn: Text, Sources, and Criticism*, Kenneth Lynn, ed. New York: Harcourt, Brace & World, 1961.

p. 110, Twain letter quoted in Lynn, ed., *Text, Sources, and Criticism.*

p. 111, Richard Chase quoted in *Twentieth Century Interpretations of Adventures of Huckleberry Finn*, Claude M. Simpson, ed. Englewood Cliffs, NJ: Prentice-Hall, 1968.

pp. 111–112, Hutchinson, Stuart. "Introduction to *The Adventures of Tom Sawyer* & *The Adventures of Huckleberry Finn*," in Bloom's Biocritiques: Mark Twain, Harold Bloom, ed. Philadelphia: Chelsea House, 2003.

p. 112, Ellison, Ralph, *Shadow and Act*, quoted in Simpson, ed., *Twentieth Century Interpretations.*

pp. 112–113, O'Meally, Robert, "Introduction," in Samuel Clemens, *Adventures of Huckleberry Finn.* New

York: Barnes and Noble Classics, 2003.

p. 113, Washington, Booker T. "Tribute to Mark Twain," *North American Review*, June 1910. BoondocksNet.com, 1995–2005. www.boondocksnet.com/twaintexts/trib_washington.html (Accessed January 18, 2005).

p. 113, Messent, Peter. *Mark Twain*. New York: St. Martin's Press, 1997.

p. 114, Schmitz, Neil. "Mark Twain's Civil War: Humor's Reconstructive Writing," in *Bloom's Biocritiques: Twain*, Bloom, ed.

p. 114, Messent. *Mark Twain*.

p. 114, DeVoto, Bernard. "The Artist as American," quoted in Simpson, ed., *Twentieth Century Interpretations*.

pp. 114–115, Marx, Leo. "Mr. Eliot, Mr. Trilling, and Huckleberry Finn," quoted in Lynn, ed. *Text, Sources, and Criticism*.

p. 115, Messent. *Mark Twain*.

p. 116, Eliot, T. S. "Introduction to *The Adventures of Huckleberry Finn*" quoted in Lynn, ed. *Text, Sources, and Criticism*.

p. 116, Smith, Henry Nash. *Mark Twain: The Development of a Writer*. Cambridge, Mass: Belknap Press, 1962.

p. 116, Marx. "Eliot, Trilling, and Finn," quoted in Lynn, ed. *Text, Sources, and Criticism*.

p. 116, O'Meally. "Introduction" in Clemens, *Huckleberry Finn*.

p. 117, Eliot, T. S. "Introduction to *The Adventures of Huckleberry Finn*" quoted in Lynn, ed. *Text, Sources, and Criticism*.

p. 118, Thompson, Charles Miner. "Mark Twain as an Interpreter of American Character." *Atlantic Monthly*, April 1897. BoondocksNet.com, 1995–2005. www.boondocksnet.com/twaintexts/mt_atlantic9704.html (accessed January 18, 2005).

p. 118, DeVoto. "The Artist as American," quoted in Simpson, ed. *Twentieth Century Interpretations*.

p. 118, Trilling, Lionel. "The Greatness of *Huckleberry Finn*," in Lynn, ed. *Text, Sources, and Criticism*.

p. 118, De Laguna, Theodore. "Mark Twain as Prospective Classic," *Overland Monthly*, April 1898. BoondocksNet.com, 1995–2005. www.boondocksnet.com/twaintexts/mt_overland9804.html (accessed January 18, 2005).

p. 119, Unsigned article. *Boston Evening Traveller*, March 5, 1885. University of Virginia, 1995. etext.lib.virginia.edu/twain/bosttrav.html (accessed January 18, 2005).

p. 119, Unsigned review. *San Francisco Daily Examiner*, March 9, 1885. University of Virginia, 1995. etext.lib. virginia.edu/twain/sfdaily.html (accessed November 22, 2004).

p. 119, Unsigned review. *Life*, February 26, 1885, quoted in Lynn, ed. *Text, Sources, and Criticism*.

p. 119, "'Huckleberry Finn' and His Critics," unsigned review. *Atlanta Constitution*, May 26, 1885. University of Virginia, 1995. etext.lib.virginia.edu/ twain/atlanta.html (accessed November 22, 2004).

p. 119, Unsigned review. *Hartford Daily Times*, March 9, 1885. University of Virginia, 1995. etext.lib.virginia.edu/twain/harttime.html (accessed November 22, 2004).

p. 119, Unsigned review. *Hartford Courant*, February 20, 1885. University of Virginia, 1995. etext.lib.virginia.edu/twain/harcour2.html (accessed November 22, 2004).

p. 119, Unsigned review. *Saturday Review*, January 31, 1885. University of Virginia, 1995. etext.virginia.edu/railton/huckfinn/satrev.html (accessed November 22, 2004).

p. 120, Paine, Albert Bigelow. *Mark Twain: A Biography, Three Volumes*, Vol. 3. New York: Harper & Brothers Publishers, 1912.

p. 122, Dempsey, Terrell. *Searching for Jim: Slavery in Sam Clemens's World*. Columbia: University of Missouri Press, 2003.

p. 123, Zwick. "Should *Huckleberry Finn* be Banned?" BoondocksNet.com, 1995–2005. www.boondocksnet.com/twainwww/essays/huck_banned9703.html (accessed January 18, 2005).

p. 123 Mencken, H. L. "The Burden of Humor." BoondocksNet.com, 1995–2005. www.boondocksnet.com/twaintexts/mencken1302.html (accessed January 18, 2005).

p. 124, Chadwick, Jocelyn. "Why Huck Finn Belongs in Classrooms," *Harvard Education Letter, Research Online,* November/December 2000. www.edletter.org/past/issues/2000-nd/huckfinn.shtml (accessed November 22, 2004).

Further Information

Books

Anderson, Frederick, ed. *A Pen Warmed-up in Hell: Mark Twain in Protest*. New York: Harper & Row, 1972.

Clemens, Samuel. *The Adventures of Huckleberry Finn* (Centennial Facsimile Edition). New York: Harper & Row, 1987.

_____. *Mark Twain's Speeches*. New York: Harper & Brothers Publishers, 1910.

Dawidziak, Mark, ed. *Mark My Words: Mark Twain on Writing*. New York: St. Martin's Press, 1996.

Howells, William Dean. *My Mark Twain: Reminiscences and Criticisms*. New York: Harper & Brothers Publishers, 1910.

Neider, Charles, ed. *The Autobiography of Mark Twain*. New York: Harper & Brothers Publishers, 1959.

Quick, Dorothy. *Enchantment: A Little Girl's Friendship with Mark Twain*. Norman: University of Oklahoma Press, 1961.

Ward, Geoffrey, Dayton Duncan, and Ken Burns. *Mark Twain: An Illustrated Biography*. New York: Alfred A. Knopf, 2001.

Web Sites

Duncan, Dayton. "Mark Twain." Corporation for Public Broadcasting.
www.pbs.org/marktwain/index.html

PBS Web site, based on the Ken Burns documentary about Mark Twain. The Web site is shown in the form of a scrapbook, with video and audio clips, photos, and quotes, along with the life story of Samuel Clemens.

Railton, Stephen, ed. "Mark Twain in His Times." Department of English, University of Virginia. 1996–2004.
etext.lib.virginia.edu/railton/index2.html

Includes the complete text of several works, as well as an electronic version of "Mark Twain's Memory Builder" game.

Waisman, Scott. "About Mark Twain." 1999.
www.geocities.com/swaisman

Includes links to many sites with information about Twain's life, works, friends, and family.

Zwick, Jim. "Mark Twain." BoondocksNet.com. 1995–2004.
www.boondocksnet.com/twainwww/index.html

Home page for Jim Zwick's BoondocksNet.com pages about Mark Twain. Links to Susy's biography, the complete text of *Huckleberry Finn*, and much more. Excellent links on criticism related to *Huck Finn* and the continuing debate on the book.

Films and Video Productions

Many film and video productions based on *The Adventures of Huckleberry Finn* have appeared in movie theaters and on television. Animated versions, television series, and plays have also been based on the book. Below is a partial list of films.

Huckleberry Finn. Dir. William Desmond Taylor. Perf. Lewis Sargent (as Huck) and Gordon Griffith (as Tom). Paramount, 1920.

Huckleberry Finn. Dir. Norman Taurog. Perf. James Durkin (as Huck) and Jackie Cooper (as Tom). Paramount, 1931.

The Adventures of Huckleberry Finn. Dir. Jack B. Hively, Michael Curtiz, and Richard Thorpe. Perf. Mickey Rooney (as Huck). MGM, 1939.

The Adventures of Huckleberry Finn. Dir. Michael Curtiz. Perf. Eddie Hodges (as Huck). MGM, 1960.

Huckleberry Finn. [Musical version of the story] Dir. J. Lee Thompson. Perf. Jeff East (as Huck). MGM, 1974.

Huckleberry Finn. [Made for television version] Dir. Robert Totten. Perf. Ron Howard (as Huck). Anchor Bay Entertainment, 1975.

The Adventures of Huckleberry Finn. [PBS mini-series] Dir. Peter H. Hunt. Perf. Patrick Day (as Huck). WGBH Boston, 1985. Monterey Home Video, 1992.

The Adventures of Huck Finn. Dir. Stephen Sommers. Perf. Elijah Wood (as Huck). Walt Disney Pictures, 1993.

_____. *Mark Twain's Speeches*. New York: Harper & Brothers Publishers, 1910.

_____. *Roughing It* (with notes and introduction by Franklin Rogers). Berkeley: University of California Press, 1972.

Dawidziak, Mark, ed. *Mark My Words: Mark Twain on Writing*. New York: St. Martin's Press, 1996.

Dempsey, Terrell. *Searching for Jim: Slavery in Sam Clemens's World*. Columbia: University of Missouri Press, 2003.

Howells, William Dean. *My Mark Twain: Reminiscences and Criticisms*. New York: Harper & Brothers Publishers, 1910.

Kaplan, Justin. *Mark Twain and His World*. New York: Simon and Schuster, 1974.

_____. *Mr. Clemens and Mark Twain: A Biography*. New York: Simon and Schuster, 1966.

Lynn, Kenneth. *Huckleberry Finn: Text, Sources, and Criticism*. New York: Harcourt, Brace & World, 1961.

Lystra, Karen. *Dangerous Intimacy: The Untold Story of Mark Twain's Final Years*. Berkeley: University of California Press, 2004.

Messent, Peter. *Mark Twain*. New York: St. Martin's Press, 1997.

Neider, Charles, ed. *The Autobiography of Mark Twain*. New York: Harper & Brothers Publishers, 1959.

Ander
Mark
1972.

Ander
Smith
Camb

Blair,
Unive

Bloor
Philac

Budd,
Bosto

Clem
tenni
1987

———
Progi

———
Twai
1917

Films and Video Productions

Many film and video productions based on *The Adventures of Huckleberry Finn* have appeared in movie theaters and on television. Animated versions, television series, and plays have also been based on the book. Below is a partial list of films.

Huckleberry Finn. Dir. William Desmond Taylor. Perf. Lewis Sargent (as Huck) and Gordon Griffith (as Tom). Paramount, 1920.

Huckleberry Finn. Dir. Norman Taurog. Perf. James Durkin (as Huck) and Jackie Cooper (as Tom). Paramount, 1931.

The Adventures of Huckleberry Finn. Dir. Jack B. Hively, Michael Curtiz, and Richard Thorpe. Perf. Mickey Rooney (as Huck). MGM, 1939.

The Adventures of Huckleberry Finn. Dir. Michael Curtiz. Perf. Eddie Hodges (as Huck). MGM, 1960.

Huckleberry Finn. [Musical version of the story] Dir. J. Lee Thompson. Perf. Jeff East (as Huck). MGM, 1974.

Huckleberry Finn. [Made for television version] Dir. Robert Totten. Perf. Ron Howard (as Huck). Anchor Bay Entertainment, 1975.

The Adventures of Huckleberry Finn. [PBS mini-series] Dir. Peter H. Hunt. Perf. Patrick Day (as Huck). WGBH Boston, 1985. Monterey Home Video, 1992.

The Adventures of Huck Finn. Dir. Stephen Sommers. Perf. Elijah Wood (as Huck). Walt Disney Pictures, 1993.

_____. *Mark Twain's Speeches*. New York: Harper & Brothers Publishers, 1910.

_____. *Roughing It* (with notes and introduction by Franklin Rogers). Berkeley: University of California Press, 1972.

Dawidziak, Mark, ed. *Mark My Words: Mark Twain on Writing*. New York: St. Martin's Press, 1996.

Dempsey, Terrell. *Searching for Jim: Slavery in Sam Clemens's World*. Columbia: University of Missouri Press, 2003.

Howells, William Dean. *My Mark Twain: Reminiscences and Criticisms*. New York: Harper & Brothers Publishers, 1910.

Kaplan, Justin. *Mark Twain and His World*. New York: Simon and Schuster, 1974.

_____. *Mr. Clemens and Mark Twain: A Biography*. New York: Simon and Schuster, 1966.

Lynn, Kenneth. *Huckleberry Finn: Text, Sources, and Criticism*. New York: Harcourt, Brace & World, 1961.

Lystra, Karen. *Dangerous Intimacy: The Untold Story of Mark Twain's Final Years*. Berkeley: University of California Press, 2004.

Messent, Peter. *Mark Twain*. New York: St. Martin's Press, 1997.

Neider, Charles, ed. *The Autobiography of Mark Twain*. New York: Harper & Brothers Publishers, 1959.

Bibliography

Anderson, Frederick, ed., *A Pen Warmed-up in Hell: Mark Twain in Protest*. New York: Harper and Row, 1972.

Anderson, Frederick, William Gibson, and Henry Nash Smith. *Selected Mark Twain–Howells Letters. 1872–1910*, Cambridge, MA: Belknap Press, 1967.

Blair, Walter. *Mark Twain & Huck Finn*. Berkeley: University of California Press, 1960.

Bloom, Harold, ed. *Bloom's BioCritiques: Mark Twain*, Philadelphia: Chelsea House Publishers, 2003.

Budd, Louis J. *Critical Essays on Mark Twain, 1867–1910*, Boston: G. K. Hall & Co., 1982.

Clemens, Samuel. *The Adventures of Huckleberry Finn* (Centennial Facsimile Edition). New York: Harper & Row, 1987.

_____. *Innocents Abroad, or The New Pilgrims' Progress*. Hartford, CT: American Publishing Co., 1871.

_____. *Life on the Mississippi. Complete Works of Mark Twain*, vol. 7. New York: Harper & Brothers Publishers, 1917.

_____. *Mark Twain's Speeches.* New York: Harper & Brothers Publishers, 1910.

_____. *Roughing It* (with notes and introduction by Franklin Rogers). Berkeley: University of California Press, 1972.

Dawidziak, Mark, ed. *Mark My Words: Mark Twain on Writing.* New York: St. Martin's Press, 1996.

Dempsey, Terrell. *Searching for Jim: Slavery in Sam Clemens's World.* Columbia: University of Missouri Press, 2003.

Howells, William Dean. *My Mark Twain: Reminiscences and Criticisms.* New York: Harper & Brothers Publishers, 1910.

Kaplan, Justin. *Mark Twain and His World.* New York: Simon and Schuster, 1974.

_____. *Mr. Clemens and Mark Twain: A Biography.* New York: Simon and Schuster, 1966.

Lynn, Kenneth. *Huckleberry Finn: Text, Sources, and Criticism.* New York: Harcourt, Brace & World, 1961.

Lystra, Karen. *Dangerous Intimacy: The Untold Story of Mark Twain's Final Years.* Berkeley: University of California Press, 2004.

Messent, Peter. *Mark Twain.* New York: St. Martin's Press, 1997.

Neider, Charles, ed. *The Autobiography of Mark Twain.* New York: Harper & Brothers Publishers, 1959.

_____. *The Selected Letters of Mark Twain*. New York: Harper & Row, 1982.

Paine, Albert Bigelow. *Mark Twain: A Biography, Three Volumes*. New York: Harper & Brothers Publishers, 1912.

Quick, Dorothy. *Enchantment: A Little Girl's Friendship with Mark Twain*. Norman: University of Oklahoma Press, 1961.

Simpson, Claude M., ed. *Twentieth Century Interpretations of Adventures of Huckleberry Finn*. Englewood Cliffs, NJ: Prentice-Hall, 1968.

Smith, Henry Nash. *Mark Twain: The Development of a Writer*. Cambridge, MA: Belknap Press, 1962.

Ward, Geoffrey, Dayton Duncan, and Ken Burns. *Mark Twain: An Illustrated Biography*. New York: Alfred A. Knopf, 2001.

Wector, Dixon. *Sam Clemens of Hannibal*. Boston: Houghton Mifflin Co., 1952.

Zwick, Jim. *Mark Twain, "Huckleberry Finn Debated,"* BoondocksNet.com. 1995-2004. www.boondocksnet.com/twainwww/hf_debate.html (accessed October 6, 2004.)

Index

Page numbers in **boldface** are illustrations, tables, and charts.
Fictional characters are shown with a (c).